REV. JŌSHŌ ADRIAN CIRLEA

SELECTED TEACHINGS OF HONEN SHONIN WITH COMMENTARY

CRAIOVA, 2024

Copyright © Adrian Gheorghe Cîrlea
All rights reserved. No part of this book may be reproduced without prior written permission from the author.

Rev. Jōshō Adrian Cîrlea (Adrian Gheorghe Cîrlea) is the representative of Jodo Shinshu Buddhist Community from Romania and founder of Amidaji branch of Jodo Shinshu Buddhism (Amidaji International Temple). He is also the author of *Buddhism of Compassion* 2007, *The Path of Acceptance – Commentary on Tannisho* 2011, *Jodo Shinshu Buddhist Teachings*, first edition 2012, *The True Teaching on Amida Buddha and His Pure Land* 2015, *The Four Profound Thoughts Which Turn the Mind Towards Amida Dharma* 2018, *The Meaning of Faith and Nembutsu in Jodo Shinshu Buddhism* 2018, *Commentary on the Sutra on the Buddha of Infinite Life* 2020, *Amida Dharma 2020, Simple Teachings on Emptiness and Buddha nature, 2020, Worshiping Amida Buddha – liturgies and ceremonies of Amidaji temple 2021, The Path Between the Thorns – the spiritual autobiography of a Jodo Shinshu Buddhist Priest, 2021, Jodo Shinshu Buddhist Teachings – 2nd revised edition, 2022, On the Monks and Nuns of Amidaji Branch of Jodo Shinshu Buddhism, 2023*

Cîrlea GheorgheAdrian
Oficiul Postal 3, Ghiseul Postal 3
Casuta postala 615
Cod poştal (postal code) 200900
Craiova, judet Dolj
Romania

phone: 0745038390
e-mail: josho_adrian@yahoo.com
website: www.amida-ji-retreat-temple-romania.blogspot.com

I dedicate this book to Adriana Cardini, Bento Abreu, Cheusa Wend, Eb Whipple, B.R. Teho, Yiju Cobi Chen, Daishin Andre Oude Wolbers, Hsu Liang Mei, Kengo Jim E, Keshin Maria Zita D'Abreu, Jose Miguel D'Abreu, Joshin David Kruemcke, Hogen David Greenhorne, Hokai Sylvie Kirsch, Horatiu Alexandru Suciu, Kishin Michael Born, Gansen John Welch, Mihaela Ungureanu, Iulia Simionca, Jiryu Doru Somesan, Jomen Kun, Judy Ng, Heng Ng, Monshin Sorinel Cont, Myoko Adelina Cont, Phyllis Latham Stoner, Rus Ilie Adrian, Tenzin Khedup, William Richard Stoner, Neal Oldham, Richard Laing, Victoria Seu and to all sentient beings in the ten directions. May they all reach the Pure Land of Amida Buddha and attain perfect Enlightenment.
Namo Amida Bu

Table of Contents

Preface..6
Honen's search for salvation..................................7
The transmission of the Nembutsu faith from Master
Shantao to Master Honen......................................11
Honen's reason for the founding of a separate Pure Land
school and my reason for founding Amidaji.............14
Honen's one-page testament..................................19
Self-power and Amida's Power..............................23
Self-power practices and teachings are not appropriate
for our times..29
The superiority of the Nembutsu Path according to
Honen Shonin..32
The uniqueness and universality of Nembutsu...........37
Do not despise other Buddhas, Dharma Gates and
Buddhist teachings because you have faith in
Amida..41
All practices are included in Nembutsu (The nun in the
Ninnaji temple)..45
Don't listen to teachers who don't believe in birth in the
Pure Land trough Nembutsu..................................50
On those who slander the exclusive Nembutsu
practitioners..53
On people who cannot be saved by Amida...............60
The meaning of "no working is true working" in relation
with our birth in the Pure Land...............................67
The protection by Amida Buddha can reach only those
who exclusively say His Name in faith....................71
There is no need to wait for the coming of Maitreya
Buddha when Amida's Primal Vow
is available here and now.......................................75

The determination of the true disciple of Amida Buddha……………………………………………...87
Honen Shonin's letter to Shōnyobō……………….89
Goodness or badness are NOT the cause of birth into the Pure Land……………………………………………100
Nembutsu is the same no matter who says it…………104
Focus on Amida's Name, not on your monkey mind……………………………………………...107
Say Nembutsu as you are……………………………110
Soldiers are saved by Amida Buddha if they entrust to Him (Honen Shonin's instructions to Samurai Taro Tadatsuma Amakasu)……………….......................116
The prostitute of Muro…………………………….124
The indiscriminative salvation offered Amida Buddha is not an encouragement to commit or justify evil……..127
Nembutsu and daily life…………………………...131
Honen said the Nembutsu as if already saved by Amida……………………………………………...135
Faith, Nembutsu and aspiration are one……………136
Say the Nembutsu with an undivided mind…………142
The number of Nembutsu recitation is not important as long as we rely on Amida's Power…………………143
Remember to say the Nembutsu…………………….149
The cause for birth into the Pure Land may appear anytime……………………………………………151
Do not mix Nembutsu with other practices………….153
Just say the Nembutsu without adding anything to it…………………………………………………...160
The thirteen contemplations are provisional practices while the Nembutsu of faith is the main Gate to the Pure Land……………………………………………...163
The need for oral instructions by a true teacher……..166

Preface

The role of a teacher is to make things simple and this is exactly what I'm trying to do through my books. I pick and choose that which is easy to understand from the many volumes of the sacred texts and organize and explain them in such a way so that both the idiot and the scholar can understand and receive faith (shinjin).

I also try to make useful connections between various Masters and their teachings. For example, in this book I show that Honen and his disciple Shinran, spoke the same language of faith and essentially taught the same teaching although sometimes the words and context are different.
Among the many sayings of Honen, I chose a few in this book and my other books, that I consider to be very important and which can serve as a standard of reading and understanding him in our Amidaji branch of Jodo Shinshu Buddhism.

I am very grateful to my Dharma friend, Gansen John Welch Sensei from Australia for proofreading the English manuscript.

Namo Amida Bu,

Jōshō Adrian Cîrlea, Amidaji temple
February 18th, 2568 Buddhist Era (2024 C.E.)

Honen's search for salvation

Here is the story of Honen's meeting with the Primal Vow in his own words[1]:

"Having a deep desire to obtain salvation, and with faith in the teachings of the various scriptures, I practiced many forms of self-discipline. There are indeed many doctrines in Buddhism, but they may all be summed up in the three learnings, namely the precepts, meditation and wisdom[2], as practiced by the adherents of the Lesser (Hinayana) and Greater Vehicles (Mahayana), and the exoteric and esoteric sects. But the fact is that I do not keep even one of the precepts, not do I attain to any one of the many forms of meditation. A certain monk said that without the observance of the sila (precepts), there is no such thing as the realization of samadhi[3]. Moreover, the heart (mind) of the ordinary unenlightened man because of his surroundings, is always liable to change, just like monkeys jumping from one branch to another. It is indeed in a state of confusion, easily moved and with difficulty controlled. In what way does right and indefectible wisdom arise? Without the sword of indefectible wisdom, how can one get free from the chains of evil passion, whence comes evil conduct? And unless one gets free from evil conduct

---

[1] Words in brackets are my own.
[2] The edition of 1925 and 1949 used the word "knowledge", but the actual meaning is wisdom, so I used it in this text.
[3] Special concentrated state of mind. Morality, meditation (Samadhi) and the development of wisdom go hand in hand on the various paths of self-power. You cannot have one without the other.

and evil passions, how shall he obtain deliverance from the bondage of birth and death? Alas! What shall I do? What shall I do? The likes of us are incapable of practicing the three disciplines of the precepts, meditation and wisdom.

And so, I enquired of a great many learned men and monks whether there is any other way of salvation than these three disciplines, that is better suited to our poor abilities, but I found none who could either teach me the way of even suggest it to me. At last, I went into the library at Kurodani at Mount Hiei, where all the scriptures were, all by myself, and with a heavy heart, read them all through. While doing so, I hit upon a passage in Shantao's Commentary on the Contemplation Sutra, which runs as follows:

'Whether walking or standing, sitting or lying, only repeat the Name of Amida with all your heart. Never cease the practice of it even for a moment. This is the very work which unfailingly issues in salvation, for it is in accordance with the Primal Vow of that Buddha'.

On reading this I was impressed with the fact, that even ignorant people like myself, by reverent meditation upon this passage, and an entire dependence upon the truth in it, never forgetting the repetition of Amida's sacred Name, may lay the foundation for that good karma which will with absolute certainty eventuate in birth into the Blissful Land. And not only was I led to believe in this teaching bequeathed by Shantao (Zendo), but also earnestly to follow the great Vow of Amida. And especially was that passage deeply inwrought into my very soul which says, 'for it is in accordance with the Primal Vow of that Buddha'".[4]

Commentary:
I would like to focus on the passage from Master Shantao that helped Master Honen entrust to Amida Buddha. He did not understand it in the sense that he must say Nembutsu in every minute or second of his life, as some might hurry to interpret it, but that there is no special inner or outer condition in which he should say the Name.

"Whether walking or standing, sitting or lying, only repeat the Name of Amida with all your heart" can be understood as saying the Nembutsu of faith in a relaxed manner without worrying about the circumstances of your life and without being attached to a specific time or posture. *"With all your heart"* means with faith, that is, with the" entrusting heart" (shinjin). *"Repeat the Name of Amida with all your heart"* is to say the Nembutsu as an expression of faith. Only this Nembutsu of faith *"is in accordance with the Primal Vow of that Buddha (Amida Buddha)"*.

This is how we should understand the passage from Master Shantao that helped Honen Shonin entrust to Amida Buddha and come in agreement with the Primal Vow.

---

[4] Honen the Buddhist Saint - His Life and Teachings, volume II, compiled by imperial order, translation by Rev Ryugaku Ishizuka and Rev Harper Havelock Coates, The Society for the Publication of Sacred Books of the World, Kyoto, 1949, p. 185-187

One who has faith in Amida Buddha will never forget to say His Name *("never forgetting the repetition of Amida's sacred Name")* but he will do it in a relaxed manner without being concerned with his state of mind, time, number of recitations, posture or any circumstance of his life, because he knows that nothing from his illusory personality can interfere with the salvation offered by Amida Buddha. In the very first moment one entrusts to Amida and says his first Nembutsu of faith he receives the merit transference from Amida Buddha that places him in the stage of nonretrogression for birth in the Pure Land. This is the meaning of *"may lay the foundation for that good karma (merit transference from Amida) which will with absolute certainty eventuate in birth into the Blissful Land"*.

For Master Honen to be in accordance with the Primal Vow was the primary goal of his life and it should be our goal too, because we are the school of the Primal Vow:

"Especially was that passage deeply inwrought into my very soul which says, 'for it is in accordance with the Primal Vow of that Buddha'".

If we are in agreement with the Primal Vow, we are carried safely to the shore of Enlightenment despite the fact that we are not capable of practicing meditation and attain samadhi, follow precepts or develop wisdom.

The transmission of the Nembutsu faith from Master Shantao to Master Honen

"One night Honen dreamed that he saw a large high mountain facing west and running north and south. A large river ran along the foot of the mountain out of the north, its waves moving towards the south. It seemed to be boundless, and on the eastern side were trackless forests. When Honen climbed half way up the mountain side and looked westward, he saw a mass of purple clouds about fifty feet from the earth flying through the air, and coming to the spot where he stood. While he was wondering at this strange sight, he noticed that countless beams of light issued from out of the clouds, and forth from these beams in all directions flew peacocks, parrots and a great variety of birds, and some of them on alighting strolled up and down the beach. Innumerable streams of light flashed forth from their bodies. After a while the whole flock flew up and went back as before into the clouds. Then the cloud, turning northward, covered the mountain and river. At this sight Honen thought to himself, 'Surely, there must be someone here about to be born into the Pure Land., when suddenly the cloud turned and stopped right in front of him, till at length it overspread the whole heavens. Then there came forth out of the cloud a monk who made towards the place where Honen was. He was clad in a golden garment from his waist downward, and in black robes from his waist upwards. Bowing respectfully with hands folded towards him, Honen said, 'And who may you be?' The monk replied, 'I am Zendo (Shantao)'. And what have you come for?' 'To show my appreciation of your

devotion to the practice and dissemination of the one and only discipline of the Nembutsu'"[5]

Commentary:
The role of that dream was to confirm Honen's teaching and to show that the transmission of the Nembutsu from Master Shantao to Master Honen was complete.
As you know, Master Shantao lived during the Tang dynasty in China, between 613 to 681, while Master Honen lived in Japan between 1133 to 1212, so they could not meet in person during their life on earth. However, as I will show in one of the chapters of this book, Honen was awakened to faith by the words of Shantao and he quoted extensively from his works, thus transmitting the essence of his teaching. As a Buddha in the Pure Land of Amida, Master Shantao noticed the Dharma work of Master Honen and he confirmed it by appearing in his dream

Of course, one does not need to have special dreams or visions in order to confirm one's faith and teaching style, so nowadays teachers or even lay people should not think there is anything wrong with them if they do not experience such things. **A person of faith always knows that he is on the right Path because faith itself gives him that certainty**. However, for future generations that dream was important to show the Nembutsu transmission from China to Japan and from Master

---

[5] Honen the Buddhist Saint - His Life and Teachings, volume II, compiled by imperial order, translation by Rev Ryugaku Ishizuka and Rev Harper Havelock Coates, The Society for the Publication of Sacred Books of the World, Kyoto, 1949, p. 205-206

Shantao to Master Honen which is why it was painted by Jodai and reached us under the name "Zendo in Honen's dream". It was a miraculous event and a confirmation from the Pure Land that what Honen taught was true and it was later used by his disciples, including Shinran, as a point of reference and a confirmation of their own teaching that they view as part of this transmission. We should remember that Shinran never considered himself to be the founder of a new school, but a transmitter of the true Pure Land teaching of Honen who himself received it from Master Shantao. Every school has a spiritual lineage and ours starts with Amida Buddha himself, then Shakyamuni – the historical Buddha[6], Nagarjuna, Vasubandhu, T'an-luan, Tao'ch'o, Shantao, Genshin, Honen, Shinran, Rennyo and various other known and unknown teachers and Masters that helped us receive this wonderful teaching.

---

[6] Also, any Buddha and Enlightened Bodhisattva can be included in the spiritual lineage of Amida Dharma (Jodo Shinshu) because all Buddhas, praise the Name of Amida Buddha and encourage us to say it in faith.

Honen's reason for the founding of a separate Pure Land school and my reason for founding Amidaji

"Honen once said: 'The reasons I founded the Jodo (Pure Land) school was that I might show the ordinary man how to be born into the Buddha's real land of compensation (hōdo). According to the Tendai sect, the ordinary man may be born into the so-called Pure Land, but that land is conceived of as a very inferior place. Although the Hossō school conceived of it as indeed a very superior place, they do not allow that the common man can be born there at all. And all the schools, though differing in many points, all agree in not allowing that the common man can be born into the Buddha's land of real compensation; while according to Zendo's (Shantao) commentary, which laid the foundation of the Jodo (Pure Land) school, it was made clear that birth into that land is possible even for the common man. But many said to me: 'You surely can promote the Nembutsu way of attaining Ojo (birth into the Pure Land) without establishing a new school. You are doing this merely out of ambition, to appear superior to others. If we ordinary people can only attain this birth, it ought to be enough to be born into the land in which the Buddha appears in His temporary body. Why do you need to talk of their reaching that land of real compensation that is occupied by the Buddhas and the highest Bodhisattvas alone?' At first sight this seems quite plausible, but on further reflection it really misses the point. Unless I start a separate school, the truth that the common man may be born into the Buddha's land of compensation will be obscured, and it will be hard to realize the deep meaning

of Amida's Primal Vow. I, therefore, in accordance with the interpretation given by Zendo (Shan-tao), unhesitatingly proclaim the doctrine of the land of real compensation. This is by no means a question of personal ambition."[7]

Commentary:
There are many ways to interpret the Pure Land teaching and the Pure Land itself, according to various schools[8]. However, Master Honen as well as Master Shinran, wanted ordinary people to understand it as the enlightened place where everybody can go without discrimination between good and evil or sages and idiots. More than this, people like us can be born directly into the center of the Pure Land, also called *"the real land of compensation"* by Honen and *"the fulfilled land of the Pure Land"* by Shinran, where we immediately become Buddhas. Contrary to this, other Masters considered that beings filled with blind passions can be born only in some kind of Nirmanakaya place in the Pure

---

[7] Honen the Buddhist Saint - His Life and Teachings, volume II, compiled by imperial order, translation by Rev Ryugaku Ishizuka and Rev Harper Havelock Coates, The Society for the Publication of Sacred Books of the World, Kyoto, 1949, p. 188-189

[8] For a detailed explanation of how various Masters in China and Japan understood the Pure Land see *The Three Pure Land Sutras – A Study and translation*, by Rev Hisao Inagaki. There Inagaki Sensei not only translates the three important sutras important for our tradition but also presents a history of the Pure Land thought in India, China and Japan. In my *Commentary on the Sutra on the Buddha of Infinite Life* I relied both on his translation as well as the translation done by Hongwanji where he also participated as a member of the translation committee.

Land, and not right in the center where Buddhas and enlightened Bodhisattvas dwell and where only the virtuous can go after death. Others considered that the Pure Land of Amida is some kind of Nirmanakaya (adaptation/temporary) land for ordinary people. Seeing the true intention of Amida Tathagata, Honen and Shinran realized that there is no difference between virtuous or unvirtuous because the cause for birth in the Pure Land is not in the spiritual capacities of beings, but in the Power of Amida Buddha himself. If one relies on that Power and says the Nembutsu of faith in Amida (the Nembutsu of the Primal Vow) then one is assured of birth in the center of the Pure Land without any discrimination. This was a true religious revolution as since then every sinner can be assured of meeting Amida, Avalokitesvara and Mahasthamaprapta face to face, upon death and birth there. From a land of spiritual elites, the Pure Land was revealed to be the easiest place to go, like a country where everybody can emigrate if they just said His Name in faith and wished to be born there. In that center of the Pure Land any former peasant and illiterate could see not a Nirmanakaya or temporary body of Amida, but Amida himself in His Sambhogakaya (Recompense) Body of Glory. Even now, disciples of later times enjoy the fruits of Honen's religious revolution.

Hundreds of years have passed since Honen to our present times when a new form of arrogant spiritual elites appeared to obstruct birth into the Pure Land for ordinary people in need of a simple faith. If in the past, their predecessors were upset that Honen cleared the door to Sukhavati for all sinners, in our times they are upset that we take the existence of Amida and His Pure Land too literally and so they try to introduce tons of alien spiritual bullshit, calling Him a symbol, fictional character or metaphor and stating that birth in the Pure Land is not to be attained after death as Honen, Shinran and Rennyo taught, but "here and now". The simple logic of salvation and of Amida's Vows who clearly mentioned the enlightened qualities of those born in the Pure Land do not matter for such scholars who are able to arrogantly ignore any doctrinal proof just to promote their new atheist and materialist reinterpretation of Jodo Shinshu Buddhism.

Just as Honen made a new Jodo (Pure Land) school, and Shinran later called his teaching the True (Shin) Pure Land (Jodo) Teaching (Shu) of Honen (Jodo Shinshu) to differentiate it from the wrong interpretations of other misguided disciples of his master, I founded Amidaji as a new branch of Jodo Shinshu to preserve and protect our Masters religious heritage against the arrogance and wrong views of today's false teachers. As Honen's actions were necessary and Shinran's clarifications of His Master's teaching were also necessary, the founding of Amidaji was too, unavoidable and necessary.

I like to call Amidaji a new branch with old roots. Like an old tree who is drying up and everybody thinks it is finished, then suddenly a new shoot appears from the underground roots, we at Amidaji begin a new chapter in a long ancient transmission of the Pure Land teaching.

Paraphrasing Honen's saying in the above passage, I say that unless I start a separate branch of Jodo Shinshu, the truth that Amida is a real, living Buddha and His Pure Land a real, enlightened place to be attained after death will be obscured. Without a new school to insist on the real, literal existence of Amida Buddha and His Pure Land, it will be hard to realize the meaning of the Primal Vow according to which there can be no faith without a real object of faith and no true aspiration for birth without a real, enlightened destination. Also, unless I start a separate branch of Jodo Shinshu, the *Larger Sutra* itself where Shakyamuni told the story of Amida will continue to be considered an invention by later monks, the general Buddhist doctrine of rebirth and life after death will also be denied and last but not least, unless I start a new branch of Jodo Shinshu Buddhism, the temples and Dharma centers will be taken over by worldly ideologies and used not for the salvation of sinners but the promotion of sin as good and beautiful.

Do not get me wrong as I do NOT think that Amidaji has the monopoly of true Dharma or that it is the only place where one can meet authentic general Buddhist and Jodo Shinshu teachings, but its founding greatly improves the chances that the Pure Land path continues to benefit sentient beings. We have our own important role to play in this Last Dharma Age and we'll stay true to our sacred mission.

Honen's one-page testament

"The method of final salvation that I have propounded is neither a sort of meditation, such as has been practiced by many scholars in China and Japan, nor is it a repetition of the Buddha's Name by those who have studied and understood the deep meaning of it. It is nothing but the mere repetition of the 'Namo Amida Butsu,' without a doubt of His mercy, whereby one may be born into the Land of Perfect Bliss.

The mere repetition with firm faith includes all the practical details, such as the threefold preparation of mind and the four practical rules. If I as an individual had any doctrine more profound than this, I should miss the mercy of the Two Honorable Ones, Amida and Shakyamuni, and be left out of the Vow of the Amida Buddha.

Those who believe this, though they clearly understand all the teachings Shakyamuni taught throughout His whole life, should behave themselves like simple-minded folks, who know not a single letter, or like ignorant nuns or monks whose faith is implicitly simple.

Thus, without pedantic airs, they should fervently practice the repetition of the Name of Amida, and that alone."[9]

---

[9] From Coates and Ishizuka, "Honen the Buddhist Saint", pp. 728-29, English translation presented in "The Buddhist Tradition in India, China and Japan" by Wm. Theodore de Bary, NY 1969, p. 331

Commentary:
First Honen said what Nembutsu Path is not, that is, not a form of meditation, not a scholarly or esoteric way. Then he explained what Nembutsu is – a simple saying/repetition of the Name in faith. If one says the Nembutsu of faith in Amida then he is sure of birth in the Pure Land after death. This saying of the Name in faith includes EVERYTHING necessary for our birth there, as well as ALL Buddhist practices. If you say the Name of Amida then you don't need to know what are *"the threefold preparation of mind and the four practical rules"* because they are automatically included and fulfilled in the Nembutsu of faith. This is why I don't even bother to explain them.

Those who try to confuse the minds of people by saying that this simple saying of the Name in faith is not enough, are not in agreement with the Primal Vow and the teaching of Shakyamuni about Amida. It is not that Amida and Shakyamuni refuse to bless them or save them, but they put themselves in a situation where these blessings and salvation cannot reach them. It is like closing one's window and stopping the rays of the sun from entering one's room.

The salvation offered by Amida takes place within the law of cause and effect. If we want to reach His Land, we need to follow the requirements mentioned in His Primal Vow. To follow the requirements of the Primal Vow (entrust to Amida Buddha, say His Name in faith and wish to be born in His Pure Land) is to enter into karmic connection with Amida (to be assured of His

salvation). Those who don't do that put themselves outside of the Primal Vow, and cannot benefit from the blessings and mercy of Shakyamuni and Amida.
Those who understand and follow this Path, no matter how smart or knowledgeable they are, should stay humble because the Nembutsu they say works only due to the Power that Amida invested in His Name. As nothing from our unenlightened personality is involved in the process of our salvation, we have no reason to consider ourselves special. We should behave like simple-minded folks because we are indeed simple-minded folks in matters related with birth and death! What can an unenlightened mind truly know about anything when compared with the mind of a Buddha? We are all ignorant until we attain perfect Enlightenment and our limited knowledge cannot save us from the ocean of samsara. This is why we should not complicate ourselves nor put pedantic airs but have a simple faith in Amida and say His Name exclusively. Why exclusively? Because in His Primal Vow, Amida did NOT mention any other thing except the Nembutsu of faith and because He knows better than us what we need in order to reach the Land that He himself created for our sake.

Shinran Shonin, who was Honen's disciple and continued His Dharma work, said in agreement with the testament of his master:

"If you imagine in me some special knowledge of a path to birth [in the Pure Land] other than the Nembutsu or of scriptural writings that teach it, you are greatly mistaken. I simply accept and entrust myself to what my

revered teacher (Honen) told me, 'Just say the Nembutsu and be saved by Amida'; nothing else is involved."[10]

For Shinran, the logic of salvation was simple:

"If Amida's Primal Vow is true, Shakyamuni's teaching cannot be false. If the Buddha's teaching is true, Shan-tao's commentaries cannot be false. If Shan-tao's commentaries are true can Honen's words be lies? If Honen's words are true, then surely what I say cannot be empty."

Amida is a real, living Buddha and a Buddha never breaks His Vow. Shakyamuni, the historical Buddha of our time, knew about Amida and His Primal Vow and He taught about them in the *Larger Sutra*, urging us to accept that teaching in faith. Then, many Masters of India, China and Japan, including Shantao and Honen, also encouraged us to have faith in Amida and say His Name. That should be enough motivation for us, disciples of modern times, to do the same.

---

[10] *Tannisho,* The Collected Works of Shinran, Shin Buddhism Translation Series, Jodo Shinshu Hongwanji-ha, Kyoto, 1997, p.662

Self-power and Amida's Power

"It is impossible to predict the length of our lives, and although we may live a long time, the past is in the end like a phantom dream.
Therefore, remember that together we will enter the same Buddha-land of Amida Buddha. Upon the lotus flower we will dispel memories of sadness in this defiled world of suffering, we will reminiscence about our past karmic connections, and we will vow to save and lead people to Enlightenment in the future. I shared the importance of this with you when we first met.

Believe deeply in the Primal Vow[11] ***of Amida Buddha;*** *do not doubt even for a moment that you will attain birth in the Pure Land; and believe that with ten recitations of Namo Amida Butsu you will definitely achieve birth in the Pure Land through the power of the Primal Vow, however much negative karma you may have. Please focus on reciting Nembutsu.*

Birth in the Pure Land will never depend upon our goodness or lack thereof. It is possible solely through the power of the Primal Vow. No matter how brilliant and admirable we may be, it is extremely difficult during this age of the Decline of the Dharma (Dharma ending age) to be born immediately into the Pure Land through one's own efforts. Because the power of the Primal Vow is the crucial factor, there is no reason that even one who is

---

[11] In the translation the term is "Essential Vow". However, I prefer to always use "Primal Vow" everywhere especially that it has the same meaning.

non-virtuous, simple and incompetent cannot attain birth in the Pure Land. **The essential condition is whether we believe in the Primal Vow of Amida Buddha**". [12]

Commentary:
Master Honen is very clear on the cause for our birth in the Pure Land, Enlightenment and the capacity to save all beings - faith in the Power of the Primal Vow: *"believe deeply in the Primal Vow of Amida Buddha".* Faith in the Primal Vow means that you believe you will go to the Pure Land *("do not doubt even for a moment that you will attain birth in the Pure Land")* if you entrust to Amida to take you there. Then you express this faith by saying His Name in a relaxed way, without worrying about the number of recitations[13] - *"believe that with ten recitations of Namo Amida Butsu you will definitely achieve birth in the Pure Land through the power of the Primal Vow".*

---

[12] The Promise of Amida Buddha: Honen's Path to Bliss, translated by Joji Atone and Yoko Hayashi, Wisdom Publications, Boston, 2011, p. 246-247

[13] Here is another passage from Honen that proves the number of recitations is not important: *"Question: Which is superior in merit: a mere single utterance of Nembutsu or ten repetitions of Nembutsu? Answer: They have the same merit with regard to birth in the Pure Land. [...] The number of recitations is not the issue. The merit of birth in the Pure Land is equal, as is clearly stated in the Primal Vow. How can there be any doubt?"*
Honen Shonin, Essential Discourse on Birth in the Pure Land through Nembutsu. *The Promise of Amida Buddha - Honen's Path to Bliss*; English translation of the Genko edition of the works of Honen Shonin - *Collected Teachings of Kurodani Shonin: The Japanese Anthology (Wago Toroku)*, translated by Joji Atone and Yoko Hayashi, Wisdom Publications, Boston, 2011, p.124-125

Shinran Shonin was also in agreement with his Master Honen:

"'Entrusting' is to be free of doubt, believing deeply and without any double-mindedness that the Tathagata's Primal Vow is true and real."[14]

Both Shinran Shonin and Honen Shonin believed deeply that birth in the Pure Land depends exclusively on the Power of Amida's Primal Vow, and not on our so-called goodness. The Power of the Primal Vow is the Power of the One who made that Vow – Amida Buddha. This is mentioned in the texts of our Masters under various titles: Power Other than self, Other Power (Tariki), etc, and is contrasted with self-power. Honen Shonin explained this difference in the following way:

"Question: Is birth in the Pure Land possible for all who recite Nembutsu?
Answer: Nembutsu relying on the Power other than self [i.e. Amida Buddha] makes birth in the Pure Land possible, but nembutsu relying on self-power will never result in birth in the Pure Land.

Question: What does Power other than self means?
Answer: Even a large boulder, placed on a ship, will be transported to the far shore in due time. This is possible not by the mobility of the stone but by the ability of the ship. Likewise, **one will see accomplishment through**

---

[14] Shinran Shonin, Notes on the Inscriptions on Sacred Scrolls, *The Collected Works of Shinran*, Shin Buddhism Translation Series, Jodo Shinshu Hongwanji-ha, Kyoto, 1997, p.493

the Power of Amida Buddha, which is referred to as the Power other than self (Other Power).

Question: What is meant by self-power?
Answer: If common mortals who possess worldly passions and are determined to rid themselves of these passions, strive to realize Enlightenment and to attain Buddhahood, even if they strive day and night, they will not be able to rid themselves of the worldly passions for very long. This is because they have been entrenched in the worldly passions of greed and anger from beginingless time. Thus, it is extremely difficult for us who are filled with the three poisons to rid ourselves of the worldly passions of ignorance. It would be as formidable a task as chipping away at Mount Meru with a tiny needle or emptying the ocean with a small ladle. Even if we were fortunate enough to chip away at Mount Meru with a needle and empty the ocean with a ladle the size of a poppy seed, innumerable eons of samsara would not help us to achieve Buddhahood. This is because we have accumulated negative karma with worldly passions. Being preoccupied by our thoughts, every moment will cause us to fall into both the three lower realms and the eight difficult conditions; and our every thought, awake and asleep, will be a bond that ties us to the six delusive worlds and the four modes of birth in the illusive worlds of transmigration. Under these circumstances, no amount of practice or study would make the attainment of Buddhahood a reality. **This**

attempt to realize Buddhahood by one's efforts is referred to as self-power."[15]

The Pure Land school is not idealistic but takes into consideration our REAL capacities and limitations. While also accepting the general doctrine of the Mahayana that all beings have Buddha nature and all can become Buddhas (discover this innate Buddha nature), Jodo Shinshu starts from our real spiritual capacities that are as good as nonexistent.

All genuine Dharma Gates have three aspects: The Basis - we all have Buddha nature, The Path - various methods to discover Buddha nature, and the Fruit (Result), which is the actual discovery of this Buddha nature. The latter is called perfect Enlightenment or Buddhahood/Nirvana. All Dharma Gates have similar basis and fruit (result), but differ in the Path which consists in various practices and teachings. Generally speaking, all these teachings and practices can be classified in two big categories: 1) self-power and 2) Other Power (Power other than self). The first implies the reliance upon our own capacity to purify ourselves of negative karma, observe precepts, do this or that meditation or practice, etc, while the latter means a total and exclusive dependence on the Power of Amida Buddha. There are also people who combine

---

[15] Honen Shonin, Essential Discourse on Birth in the Pure Land through Nembutsu, *The Promise of Amida Buddha - Honen's Path to Bliss*; English translation of the Genko edition of the works of Honen Shonin - *Collected Teachings of Kurodani Shonin: The Japanese Anthology (Wago Toroku)*, translated by Joji Atone and Yoko Hayashi, Wisdom Publications, Boston, 2011, p.119-121

dependency on their self-power with Amida's Power (Shinran calls this "self-power within Other Power") but by doing this they actually cannot be put in the category of genuine Other Power because Other Power or Power other than self means to rely EXCLUSIVELY and TOTALLY on Amida Buddha for our birth in the Pure Land, without thinking even for a second that we can add anything to this goal from our unenlightened personality.

To think that you can attain the fruit of the Path (Buddhahood) through relying completely or partially on your self-power is to be ignorant of your limited capacities and the influence of the habitual karma from the past. It means, as I often say, to behave like a drug addict who pretends that he can give up drugs instantly after twenty or more years of addiction. Just like he might end up taking a super dose after a few hours of abstinence, we can also fall prey to just one moment of anger and lose all the karmic good that we have accumulated in many months or years of self-power practice. This is why Honen said that if we depend on our own limited capacities and ever-changing personalities then *"every moment will cause us to fall into the three lower realms"*. Instead of attaining liberation *"our every thought, awake and asleep, will be a bond that ties us to the six delusive worlds"*.

The Pure Land teaching sheds light on our limitations and puts us in the right place. It is the mirror into which we see ourselves as we really are and makes us realize we need Amida's helping hand.

Self-power practices and teachings are not appropriate for our times

"Regardless of whether it is of Mahayana Buddhism or Hinayana Buddhism, we cannot endure the training in these sacred teachings of the four vehicles, as they are not appropriate teachings for our present time……It is unnecessary to state here that in this period of the decline of Dharma (the Last Dharma Age), pursuit of these achievements is almost impossible, especially for those of us with minimal capabilities…..It goes without saying that in the present day, while it is still the period of the decline of the Dharma (the Last Dharma Age), let alone during the periods of the true Dharma (the Right Dharma Age) and the semblance of the Dharma (the Semblance Dharma Age), no being is excluded from birth in the Pure Land."[16]

Commentary:
As I previously explained, the capacities of beings in the Last Dharma Age are no longer in agreement with the self-power practices and teachings taught in the Right Dharma Age. When the teachings and practices are not in accord with the capacities of beings it means that they are as good as non-existent. Those who still seem to achieve high spiritual states through them or even Enlightenment, are actually high level or enlightened

---

[16] *The Promise of Amida Buddha - Honen's Path to Bliss*; English translation of the Genko edition of the works of Honen Shonin - *Collected Teachings of Kurodani Shonin: The Japanese Anthology (Wago Toroku)*, translated by Joji Atone and Yoko Hayashi, Wisdom Publications, Boston, 2011, p.95-97

Bodhisattvas in disguise coming in this world in various Buddhist schools to keep on the Buddhist Path, by their own example, those who cannot yet entrust to Amida's Primal Vow. Because they are already enlightened or on one of the ten stages (bhumis), they did not actually start from zero or from the low-level capacities of people in our age. All their so-called achievements are just a play to help self-power Buddhists, until a better age (the ages of future great Buddhas) will arrive and beings will be able again to easily advance on any Buddhist Path. However, until then, the only Dharma method that is suitable for any age and any spiritual capacities is that offered by the Primal Vow of Amida Buddha. To say His Name in faith is effective in the Right Dharma Age, the Semblance Dharma Age and the Last Dharma Age in which we are living now. Even after this Dharma ending Age[17], when there will be no other Buddhist teaching available, the Nembutsu of faith will still be able to liberate beings. This is why although any Buddhist path is wonderful and perfect in itself, only the Vehicle of the Primal Vow is universal and supreme in the sense that it can lead all beings to final liberation without discriminating between their spiritual capacities.

Because to help all beings attain Buddhahood is the goal of any Buddha, and Amida's Primal Vow is the easiest Path towards this, all Buddhas encourage us to entrust to Amida and say His Name in faith. No matter that each Buddha has various teachings and practices associated

---

[17] The last Dharma Age will last around ten thousand years according to some scriptural sources.

with them that they themselves teach for those who can't yet entrust to Amida, they all support and praise Amida's Primal Vow and Amida's Name.

All the methods of the Hinayana and Mahayana, including the Vajrayana, were specially made by the Buddhas for those who cannot yet entrust to Amida. Some people attained liberation through them in the Right Dharma Age and very few in the Semblance Dharma Age. However, in the Last Dharma Age and the dark period after it, no ordinary person like me or you can achieve liberation through them, so we should better admit our limitations and accept Amida's helping hand.

The superiority of the Nembutsu Path according to Honen Shonin

Honen had the following dialogue with Shinjakubo from Harima:

"'Suppose two imperial orders were sent out, one for the western and the other for the eastern provinces. What would you think, if the one intended for the western were by mistake taken to the eastern provinces, or vice versa? Would the people observe them?' After some thought Shinjakubo replied: 'Even though they were imperial orders, how would it be possible for the people to observe them?' 'Right you are', said Honen. 'Now by the two imperial orders, I mean the teachings we inherit from Shakyamuni belonging to the so-called three periods, that of the Right Dharma Age, the Semblance Dharma Age and the Last Dharma Age[18]. The practice of the so-called Holy Path (Shōdō), belongs to the periods of the Right Dharma Age and the Semblance Dharma Age, and is only attainable by men of superior capacity and wisdom. Let us call this the imperial order to the western provinces. The practice of the so-called Pure Land (Jodo) belongs to the degenerate age when the Dharma[19] has fallen into decay, in which even the most

---

[18] The edition of 1925 and 1949 used the words "perfect Law, the imitation of the Law and the ending of the Law". These have the same meaning with the Right Dharma Age, the Semblance Dharma Age and the Last Dharma Age, which are present day translations of the same terms. This is why I prefer to use the later.

[19] The edition of 1925 and 1949 used the word "Law" for the Dharma.

worthless may find the way of salvation. Let us liken this to the imperial order to the eastern provinces. So, it would never do to confuse these two paths, only one of which is suited to all three periods. I once discussed the doctrines of the Holy Path (path of self-power) and of the Pure Land with several scholars at Ōhara, and admitted that they both are equally Buddhistic, just as both horns of an ox are equally his own. I went on to show that from the standpoint of human capacity, my doctrine of the Pure Land is much superior and has had by far the greater success. Though the Holy Path is indeed profound, it belongs to an age already past, and is not suited to men of the present day, and while the Pure Land seems shallow it really is just the thing for our generation. When I thus won in the argument, the audience applauded, deeply convinced of the truth of the saying: 'In the period of the Last Dharma Age, which last ten thousand years, all other sutras shall perish, but the one teaching of Amida alone shall remain to bless men and endure.'" [20]

Commentary:
The fragment above is very clear and doesn't need too much of an explanation. I just want to insist a little on this sentence: *"my doctrine of the Pure Land is much superior and has had by far the greater success"* and on the last one: *"in the period of the Last Dharma Age, which last ten thousand years, all other sutras shall*

---

[20] Honen the Buddhist Saint - His Life and Teachings, volume II, compiled by imperial order, translation by Rev Ryugaku Ishizuka and Rev Harper Havelock Coates, The Society for the Publication of Sacred Books of the World, Kyoto, 1949, p. 189-190

perish, but the one teaching of Amida alone shall remain to bless men and endure.'"

Here by using the term "superior" Master Honen does not wish to slander self-power Buddhist teachings and practices, nor to insult their followers. **What he meant by superiority is the easiness and universality of the Pure Land Path.** As we know, the goal of any Buddha is to bring ALL beings to the attainment of perfect Enlightenment. I repeat – ALL beings, not just the spiritual elite, not only those capable to retire in a monastery and practice austerities, but ALL beings, including the most evil and ignorant person, including YOU, the reader of these lines who cannot sit all day in meditation. What method among all invented by any Buddha is really capable to do this if not the Primal Vow of Amida? Any other teaching and practice in which self-power is involved requires various spiritual qualities in order to be effective, while Amida Buddha asks nothing but a simple faith in His Salvific Power. The idiot and the wise, the sinner and the moral person, the householder and the celibate can equally achieve birth in the Pure Land of Amida if they entrust to Him, say His Name in faith and wish to be born there. No special capacity is required, no virtues, no nothing. **This is why this it is called superior, because it fulfils the main reason for all Buddhas coming to this world – to bring ALL beings to final liberation.**

And it has the greatest success, as Honen said, because it does not depend on us. If to reach a distant town requires specific skills that only some possess, there will be people who will not be able to arrive there, but if a luxurious bus is offered freely to all, without even the need to buy a ticket or be dressed appropriately, then anybody who jumps in the bus will be taken safely to the destination.

The perishing of the sutras in the Last Dharma Age with the exception of the *Larger Sutra* on Amida Buddha means that even if we can still read and find many types of sutras in our libraries or online, nobody can actually use the self-power practices described there to attain perfect Enlightenm
ent (like Shakyamuni) during the present life. Thus, they are as good as non-existent for this Last Dharma Age. So, if someone would argue that the internet is filled with many sutras, we can simply tell them: "ok, then go and attain Buddhahood through them". The words of Honen are similar with those of Shinran Shonin from the *Shozomatsu Wasan*:

*"...the teachings that Sakyamuni left behind
Have all passed into the naga's palace."*

To "pass into the naga's palace" means not being effective or being as good as non-existent. He also said, in the same spirit as his Master Honen:

*"Although we have the teachings of Sakyamuni,
There are no sentient beings who can practice them;
Hence, it is taught that in the last Dharma-age,
Not a single person will attain Enlightenment through them."*

"Not a single person will attain Enlightenment through them" is a very strong statement but Shinran and Honen did not appear in this world to be politically correct. Not a single person can effectively practice[21] any Buddhist Path other than the Nembutsu of faith in Amida Buddha. And even that is not actually a practice but a simple saying of His Name.

---

[21] To practice effectively in the case of self-power practices means to attain perfect Enlightenment like Shakyamuni in this life. To practice effectively in the case of Amida centered Path is to say the Nembutsu of faith in this life and attain perfect Enlightenment in the Pure Land after death.

The uniqueness and universality of Nembutsu

"When we say that the Jodo (Pure Land) is superior to all other sects, and that the Nembutsu is superior to all other religious disciplines, we mean that it provides salvation for all classes of sentient beings. Of course, meditation upon the Absolute, heart longing for perfect knowledge (Bodhi), the reading and reciting of the Mahayana Sutras, the mystic practices of the Shingon, the meditation of the Tendai, and so on, all belong to the Dharma of the Buddhas, reveal their superiority, and tell us how to cross over the sea of birth and death. And yet on the other hand, they are quite beyond the capacity of people living in these later degenerate times. After the ten thousand years of these latter evil days have passed, the average length of human life is to be shortened to ten years, and many will degenerate so that they will be guilty of the ten evil deeds and the five deadly sins, and yet the whole of them old and young, male and female, all without exception, are included within the scope of that Primal Vow, and are given the assurance that they will be cared for and never forsaken, if they will but repeat the Nembutsu ten times, or even once. This is why we insist that the Nembutsu quite outrivals all other sects and disciplines."[22]

---

[22] Honen the Buddhist Saint - His Life and Teachings, volume V, compiled by imperial order, translation by Rev Ryugaku Ishizuka and Rev Harper Havelock Coates, The Society for the Publication of Sacred Books of the World, Kyoto, 1949, p. 734-735

Commentary:
As we see in the above text, Honen used the word "superiority" two times, first in relation with the Pure Land Nembutsu school *("the Jodo is superior to all other sects")* and second while referring to other Mahayana schools who also *"reveal their superiority"* because they too have methods for crossing the ocean of birth and death. This aspect and his next explanations clarify that his intention was not to slander other Buddhist schools and Dharma Gates but to show the universal applicability of the Nembutsu and Amida's Primal Vow versus the limited relevance of other practices. Shinran was also in agreement with his Master Honen, when he said:

„The two forms of relevance are: first, limited relevance; second, universal relevance. The Pure Land is the teaching of universal relevance."[23]

While all Buddhist practices and methods are good and excellent because they were taught by the Buddhas, not all of them can be followed by everybody as some require special capacities, time, discipline and wisdom. Not many can do complicated visualizations, meditate on the Absolute (Buddha nature), sit in a rigorous posture, do the various mystic practices of the esoteric schools or even spend their entire time in studying and reciting Mahayana sutras, etc. On the other hand, anybody can get the simple "come as you are" message of Amida

---

[23] Shinran Shonin, *Lamp for the Latter-Ages*, letter 8, *The Collected Works of Shinran*, Shin Buddhism Translation Series, Jodo Shinshu Hongwanji-ha, Kyoto, 1997, p.535

Buddha, say His Name in faith and rely on Him to be born in His Pure Land after death.

Nothing is easier than saying Namo Amida Bu (I take refuge in Amida Buddha/Homage to Amida Buddha). This Nembutsu is not a religious discipline in the sense that it doesn't need to be said while sitting in a specific posture of the body and with a special attitude of mind. The Name of Amida Buddha can be said in many forms, any circumstance, no matter if we sit, stand up, walk, lay down, and even with a scattered mind. This is because the efficacy of Nembutsu does not depend on us but on Amida's power invested in His Name. Even the word "recitation" is not quite perfect, although we use it, when referring to Nembutsu. This is because recitation still means a certain discipline in the pronunciation and sound which is not required by Amida who, in His Primal Vow, used the expression "say my Name". Thus, Nembutsu is not actually a discipline or a practice (although we also use this word sometimes) like that of other schools where a mantra must be recited in a certain way and with a specific attitude of mind or for as many times as possible.

Even those living in the last Dharma age (Mappo) like us, or during the period that will follow it in which human life's expectancy will decrease to ten years due to many wars, famine and epidemics, can still be saved if they only say Namo Amida Bu[24] once. I repeat – only

---

[24] For a good understanding of the concept of Mappo please read chapters "The Three Dharma Ages" and "Jodo Shinshu – the only

one Nembutsu of faith can save us from the ocean of birth and death! What can be easier than that? Here is why *"the Nembutsu quite outrivals all other sects and disciplines"*.

If we find it hard to focus on self-power practices in our modern times, how more difficult could that be when people live only ten years of unimaginable suffering! This is the so-called superiority Honen was talking about and which I also call uniqueness or universality of the Nembutsu Path.

Methods can be measured after their level of applicability to all times and circumstances. Cars that go only on good highways may be wonderful, but those who can cross any terrain are better due to their universal efficacy. The Buddhist paths that bring to Enlightenment only those who can successfully practice visualization and meditation, observe precepts and have a perfect moral life are also true and splendid but they are not universal in the sense that they do not save the sinner and the idiot. And I am sorry to say it again, as I know many would not like it, but we are all sinners and idiots when compared with a Buddha, so we all need Amida's helping hand.

---

effective path in this last Dharma age" from my book *Jodo Shinshu Buddhist Teachings* 2nd revised edition, p 137-151.

Do not despise other Buddhas, Dharma Gates and Buddhist teachings because you have faith in Amida

Honen Shonin said:

"Just because one relies solely upon Amida Buddha and believes only in Nembutsu, do not make light of the compassionate vows of various Buddhas and Bodhisattvas, or think ill of and slander wondrous sutras such as the Lotus Sutra or the Perfection of Wisdom Sutra. The karma of defaming myriad Buddhas and of doubting and slandering many holy teachings is not in harmony with the heart of Amida Buddha. Such actions would certainly exclude one from His compassionate Vow even if one recites Nembutsu".[25]

Commentary:
This excellent teaching of Honen Shonin is fundamental to our Amidaji school.

To believe in the existence of Amida while denying the existence of other Buddhas or to accept the *Larger Sutra* on Amida while denigrating other Mahayana sutras is a karmic and logical impossibility. One who denies the existence of other Buddhas cannot have the good karma of becoming open to the Primal Vow of Amida. He also

---

[25] Honen Shonin, *Instruction in seven articles, The Promise of Amida Buddha - Honen's Path to Bliss*; English translation of the Genko edition of the works of Honen Shonin - Collected Teachings of Kurodani Shonin: The Japanese Anthology (Wago Toroku), translated by Joji Atone and Yoko Hayashi, Wisdom Publications, Boston, 2011, p.136-137

cannot be guided by other Buddhas and Enlightened Bodhisattvas towards Amida.

More than this, to denigrate other Buddhas and their vows and methods or other sutras can be considered an act of slandering the right Dharma which leads to self-exclusion from the Primal Vow. This is logical because if one denies the existence of other Buddhas how can he accept the existence of Amida? Or if he slanders their sutras and methods of salvation, how can he take as real and effective Amida's method or the sutra about Amida? For example, if one does not believe in the existence of human beings, how can he believe in your existence, the reader of these lines? It is the same with the Buddhas and their methods. If one does not believe in the existence of transcendent Buddhas and Enlightened Bodhisattvas, how can he believe in Amida, or if one denies the authenticity of Mahayana sutras, how can he accept the *Larger Sutra* which is itself part of the Mahayana canon? Please remember the explanations of Master T'an-luan of the characteristics of slandering the right Dharma: *"Saying there is no Buddha, no Buddha-Dharma"*– that is, to deny the existence of any Buddha, not only Amida, and to deny the various methods of the Buddha Dharma, not only Amida Dharma.

Shinran Shonin also said: *"If one speaks slightingly of the Buddhas, then one is surely a person who does not entrust oneself to the Nembutsu and who does not say Amida's Name"*[26].

---

[26]Shinran Shonin, *A Collection of Letters*, Letter 4, The *Collected Works of Shinran*, Shin Buddhism Translation Series, Jodo Shinshu Hongwanji-ha, Kyoto, 1997, p.563

One who slanders other Buddhas, Enlightened Bodhisattvas and Dharma Gates automatically self excludes himself from the salvation of Amida Buddha and has no place in our Amidaji sangha.

All Buddhas and Enlightened Bodhisattvas have been our spiritual parents and guides since the beginingless time, helping us in many ways to come closer and closer to Amida's Primal Vow, so as I said, it is a karmic impossibility for one who has faith in Amida to slander them and deny their existence:

"Sakyamuni and all the other Buddhas
Are truly our compassionate father and mother.
With various compassionate means they lead us to awaken
Supreme shinjin (faith in Amida) that is true and real."[27]

Also, a person of faith does not pick and choose what he likes from the Buddha Dharma and denies what doesn't fit with the worldly ideologies of his time. A true follower of Amida accepts in faith even those teachings of Shakyamuni that he cannot follow due to his blind passions and limitations. Thus, he will not deny the Buddhist moral precepts because he is not a moral person, especially when he knows that he is saved as he is by Amida Buddha, nor will he deny rebirth and life after death because atheism and materialism is a popular trend of his time. He acknowledges his limitations and

---

[27] Shinran Shonin, Hymn of the Two Gateways of Entrance and Emergence, The Collected Works of Shinran, Shin Buddhism Translation Series, Jodo Shinshu Hongwanji-ha, Kyoto, 1997, p.629

does not criticize what he does not yet understand but patiently waits for the moment when he will know everything as a Buddha in the Pure Land of Amida.

The disciple of Amida and all Buddhas is relaxed with the Dharma and finds no conflict between one's mind and the Buddha's teaching. He knows that if Shakyamuni was right when He taught about Amida Buddha, then He was not mistaken whenever He shared other teachings. Unfortunately, there are so many nowadays in the Western world, even among those who wear the robes and kesa of the Nembutsu faith, who are always at war with the Dharma, constantly trying to change it or adapt it to their limited unenlightened views. It is a pity that their karma for birth in human world is spent in vain as what they actually do is *"doubting and slandering many holy teachings"* and are *"not in harmony with the heart of Amida Buddha"*.

All practices are included in Nembutsu
(The nun in the Ninnaji temple)

"There was once a nun in the Ninnaji temple who came to Honen, and with a tone of sadness in her voice, said she had made a vow to read the Hokke Sutra (Lotus Sutra) a thousand times over. She had already finished reading it seven hundred times, but as she was now getting quite old, she did not know how to obtain the merit of doing the rest. Then Honen said, 'You have indeed done well despite your age to read it over seven hundred times. As to the other three hundred, the best thing to do is to apply your whole mind to one thing, and that is the practice of the Nembutsu'.
She took his advice, gave up the reading, and did nothing but call upon the sacred Name all the rest of her life, till she at last attained Ojo (birth in the Pure Land).

In the village of Shiraku, in the province of Tango, there was a cloister called Mirokuji, the abbot of which was formerly a Tendai scholar, who afterwards, on retiring from his priestly office, became a disciple of Honen, devoting himself exclusively to the Nembutsu practice. He lived at Tomino-koji, Gojo Bomon (in Kyoto). One day, when taking a mid-day nap, he had a dream, in which he thought he saw purple clouds in the sky, and a nun in the midst of them with a face brimming all over with smiles, who said, 'Through the teaching of Honen Shonin I have attained birth into the Pure Land. I was once a nun in the Ninnaji temple'.
With this he awoke. After a while he visited Honen at his residence at Kujo, and told the dream he had had, saying

it must have been a mental illusion. Honen, after a little reflection said, 'Well, there was such a person as this. And late he thought he would send a messenger to the Ninnaji temple, but as it was already dark, did not send till the next morning, when he told the messenger, 'Today as I had business this way, I have just dropped in. Has anything special happened?' As the messenger went and made the call, he was told that the nun had died the day before at the hour of the horse. Is this not a strange phenomenon?"[28]

My commentary:
As we can see above, Master Honen did not denigrate the self-power practice the nun chose to do before coming to him, nor did he say that the recitation/reading of the *Lotus Sutra* is wrong. He didn't do that because he knew that the *Lotus Sutra* represents a genuine Dharma Gate taught by Shakyamuni Buddha. What Honen did was to emphasize the difficulty of that practice for a person her age and he kindly guided her to the Nembutsu of faith who contains the merits of all practices and fulfills all spiritual aspirations. We have to remember again and again how he and Master Shan-tao explained the merits contained in Amida's Name. The following is a passage I keep close to my heart and show it to people who are afraid that by turning to Amida for refuge they somehow abandon their previous vows, when actually the saying of the Nembutsu is the surest way to fulfill

---

[28] Honen the Buddhist Saint - His Life and Teachings, volume III, compiled by imperial order, translation by Rev Ryugaku Ishizuka and Rev Harper Havelock Coates, The Society for the Publication of Sacred Books of the World, Kyoto, 1949, p. 378-379

them and their aspiration to attain Buddhahood for the benefit of all beings[29]:

"The Japanese designation for Amitabha - Amida - consists of only three characters (A-MI-DA). Within this Name, however, is the merit of the inner realization of Tathagata Amida and His external activities, as well as **the merit of Buddha Shakyamuni's extremely profound teachings (Lotus Sutra included!)**, *which are as numerous as the grains of sand in the Ganges. Who can fathom this?*

Master Shan-tao, in the chapter 'Essentials of the Commentary' of the 'Commentary on the Meditation Sutra', interpreted this Name thus:

'The Chinese term for Amida Buddha, 'A-mi-t'o-fo', is a transliteration of the language of India. It was interpreted into Chinese as 'Enlightened One Whose Life Is Immeasurable (Wu-liang-shou-chiao)'. 'Immeasurable Life (Wu-liang-shou) points to the Dharma, and 'Enlightened One (chiao)' is a person. Both the Dharma and the person are combined into 'Enlightened One Whose Life Is Immeasurable'. Accordingly, He is referred to as 'A-mi-t'o-fo'.' […]

Therefore, **all of the merits of the teachings (Lotus Sutra included!),** *the meditative practices on the phenomenal aspect of reality and the noumenal principle, the unmatched power acquired through*

---

[29] Words in brackets are my own.

meditation and wisdom, the wisdom of inner realization, and the merit of external activities, as well as all of the virtues and undefiled Enlightenment of Tathagata Amida, Bodhisattva Avalokitesvara, Bodhisattva Mahasthamaprapta, Bodhisattva Samanthabhadra, Bodhisattva Manjusri, Bodhisattva Ksitigarbha, Nagarjuna, and the Bodhisattvas[30] *and Sravakas*[31] *of the Pure Land* **are encompassed in the three characters of the Name of Amida**. *This being so,* **would there be any Dharma not included in the teaching for birth in the Pure Land?***"*[32]

To say that all Dharma Gates are included in the teaching for birth in the Pure Land *("would there be any Dharma not included in the teaching for birth in the Pure Land?")* means that the Primal Vow of Amida and His Name brings all beings to the attainment of

---

[30] Bodhisattvas in the Pure Land refer to those who attained Enlightenment in the Pure Land and are now Buddhas who manifest as Bodhisattvas. For a better understanding of this idea read chapter "The qualities of Bodhisattvas in the audience" from my book, *Commentary on the Sutra on the Buddha of Infinte Life*, Dharma Lion Publications, Craiova, 2020, p. 24, https://amida-ji-retreat-temple-romania.blogspot.com/2019/01/commentary-on-sutra-on-buddha-of.html

[31] Here "sravaka" is not used with the sense of a Hinayana follower, but of a close enlightened disciple of Amida in His Pure Land.

[32] Honen Shonin, *Commentary on the Three Sutras of Pure Land Buddhism, The Promise of Amida Buddha - Honen's Path to Bliss, The Promise of Amida Buddha - Honen's Path to Bliss*; English translation of the Genko edition of the works of Honen Shonin - *Collected Teachings of Kurodani Shonin: The Japanese Anthology (WagoToroku)*, translated by Joji Atone and Yoko Hayashi, Wisdom Publications, Boston, 2011, p.81-82

Buddhahood which is, in fact, the goal of all Dharma Gates and teachings, including the *Lotus Sutra*.

By guiding the nun to Nembutsu, Honen changed her mind from the pursuit of accumulating merits through self-power effort to the already available storehouse of infinite virtues that Amida concentrated in His Holy Name. By saying the Nembutsu of Faith she automatically received the merits of the *Lotus Sutra* and became a splendid Buddha in the Pure Land of Amida.

Don't listen to teachers who don't believe in birth in the Pure Land through Nembutsu

"It is indeed lamentable and regrettable that there are those who say birth in the Pure Land is impossible. Please, do not ever be swayed by such words, even if the speakers are wise and honorable. They may be people who are learned and respected in their individual paths of endeavor, but the instructions of those with different understandings and practices will be troublesome for those who are aspiring for birth in the Pure Land. These proponents of other practices are referred to as 'undesirable teachers who will serve to distance the aspirants from their karmic relationship with Amida Buddha.' You must not lend an ear to such misguided people but continue to rely steadfastly on the Primal Vow for birth in the Pure Land".[33]

Commentary:
We cannot understand, at the level we are now as unenlightened beings, every detail of all the Buddhist paths, especially since we did not create them. We are like travelers lost in a dangerous jungle looking for the safety of the beach. Because we do not fly and cannot see the jungle from above, we need to choose one Path among the many that were made for us by the Guide.

---

[33] *The Promise of Amida Buddha - Honen's Path to Bliss*; English translation of the Genko edition of the works of Honen Shonin - *Collected Teachings of Kurodani Shonin: The Japanese Anthology (Wago Toroku)*, translated by Joji Atone and Yoko Hayashi, Wisdom Publications, Boston, 2011, p.248

The Buddhas see and understand with their divine eyes and unobstructed wisdom the entire samsaric jungle and are able to cut through it various Paths, each with its own specific elements to guide various types of people with different understandings and affinities. Thus, they teach the Zen Paths, the Esoteric Paths, the so and so Buddhist Path, and the Pure Land Path of exclusive reliance on the Primal Vow of Amida Buddha. Travelers who choose to walk on one Path cannot give indications to those who walk on another that they themselves do not see, nor follow. A teacher who plays smart with many Dharma Gates is like one who lived all his life in the mountains and walked only on mountain paths, and he insists on giving indications to those who walk through the desert. To express opinions about Amida Buddha and His Pure Land when one does not have faith in Him is like a blind person talking about things he never saw. Yes, dear friends, as long as one has not said the Nembutsu of faith he cannot know the Path of the Primal Vow and cannot teach others about it. More than this, it is a sign of spiritual arrogance to say to an Amida devotee that birth in the Pure Land is impossible or that our Nembutsu Path does not work. Really, how can a teacher of a different Path know that Nembutsu does not work, as long as he never entrusted himself to Amida, nor had the aspiration for birth in His Land?

I've seen a tendency in some contemporary teachers of other Buddhist Paths to interpret various elements of our tradition through the concepts of their own Dharma Gate. This causes a lot of confusion and leads to false views like the idea of Pure Land is not to be found after death, but here and now or in the mind, etc. Sometimes well-educated scholars who wear the robes and kesas of Jodo Shinshu but in their hearts are ashamed to belong to a school of simple faith, also contribute to this confusion. They play nice with such teachers from other Dharma Gates hoping to be seen as more elevated than us peasants, who believe that we'll go to the Pure Land after death. These people don't like Jodo Shinshu as it is, I mean as it was transmitted by Honen, Shinran and Rennyo, but want it to be more Zen-like or in agreement with other teachings and even worldly philosophies.

My heart advice to my fellow simple-minded peasants is to have eyes and ears only for the exclusive requirements of the Primal Vow if they want to enter into karmic relationship with Amida Buddha and be sure of reaching His Pure Land. **Birth there is possible because Amida said is possible and Shakyamuni confirmed it together with our great Masters of the past.** Only fools whose life in human form is spent in vain would trust the words of unenlightened teachers of self-power paths and not Amida and Shakyamuni!

"If those who entrust to me, say my Name, and wish to be born in my Land will not go there, then it means I am not a Buddha" - this is the essence of Amida's Primal Vow. Because He is a Buddha, He will never break His promise.
Namo Amida Bu

On those who slander the exclusive Nembutsu practitioners

Honen Shonin said in *An Outline of Nembutsu*:

"It is even more unfortunate that there are many who insult and deride the exclusive practitioners of Nembutsu today. These unfortunate circumstances were foretold by incarnate Buddhas and Bodhisattvas a long time ago. Accordingly, Bodhisattva Manjusri stated, 'Nonvirtuous beings in the future world will recite the Name of Amida Buddha in the West, become detached from the delusive worlds of saṃsara by relying on the Primal Vow, and be born in the Pure Land through the depth of their sincere heart.'

In the Hymns of the Nien-fo Liturgy, Master Shan-tao thus stated:
'At the very moment when the World-Honored One [Buddha Shakyamuni] was coming to the end of His sermon, He entrusted to Sariputra with great care the Name of Amida Buddha[34].
Over time, after the death of Buddha Shakyamuni, the five defilements proliferated, and many people began to slander the teaching of Nembutsu. Monastics and lay people alike began to dislike the teaching of Nembutsu and ceased listening to it. This gave rise to the poison of anger, and when they saw Nembutsu practitioners, they struggled to incite intrigue and create grudges. Such

---

[34] I think that Master Shan-tao refers here to the *Smaller Amida Sutra (Amidakyo)* where Shakyamuni speaks to Shariputra alone.

people seem blind by nature and have no intrinsic goodness. Destroying the teaching designed for the instantaneous realization of Enlightenment, they will sink into the three lower realms for a long time. They will never be released from the three lower realms, even though innumerable eons pass, more numerous than the number of particles released in the explosion of the earth.

The Sutra of Universal Enlightenment states: 'If a good man and woman listen to the teaching of Nembutsu, are overwhelmed both with sorrow at their state of ignorance and with unspeakable elation at the promise of birth in the Pure Land, and attempt to escape from the three lower realms, then it is clear that they have already cultivated the path leading to Enlightenment in a previous life[35]. Conversely, if a person does not rejoice even after listening to the teaching, it is a sign that he has just emerged for the first time from the three lower realms.'

Those who criticize and slander the teaching of Nembutsu are merely obsessed with illogical reasons, which are not worthy of debate."[36]

---

[35] They have "good from the past" as Rennyo Shonin explained.

[36] *The Promise of Amida Buddha - Honen's Path to Bliss*; English translation of the Genko edition of the works of Honen Shonin - *Collected Teachings of Kurodani Shonin: The Japanese Anthology (Wago Toroku)*, translated by Joji Atone and Yoko Hayashi, Wisdom Publications, Boston, 2011, p.150-151

Commentary:
"'Nonvirtuous beings in the future world" refer to us, ordinary people of blind passions living in the Last Dharma Age. We become assured of liberation from samsara *("become detached from the delusive worlds of saṃsara")* by saying the Nembutsu of faith in accordance with the Primal Vow of Amida Buddha.

There is a reason why this precious teaching was slandered in the past and is still slandered today. By being slandered today I refer to those belonging to other Paths[37] who look down on us for having a teaching too simple to be true, but also to false teachers who wear the robes and kesas of Nembutsu faith in various branches of Jodo Shinshu and who deny the existence of Amida Buddha by calling Him a myth, symbol and metaphor or who do not admit that the Pure Land is a real enlightened place to be attained after death. They too consider our devotional approach and simple faith to be ridiculous and dismiss it as folk religion.

Why there are so many wrong views about a Path like ours? Because it is the quickest way through which all beings (not only the spiritual elites) can attain Liberation. The Primal Vow is *"the teaching designed for the instantaneous realization of Enlightenment"* after death and birth in the Pure Land, so it's too easy to be left without complications. Various Maras and evil

---

[37] Not all followers of other schools are like this, of course. Here I refer only to a category of infatuated and self-deluded people.

spirits who don't want people to escape their grasp, are even more determined to possess and influence those who can infiltrate and stop the spreading of the Primal Vow than those who teach self-power methods which are hard to follow anyway in this Last Dharma Age. However, the Path of faith in the real, living Amida Buddha will endure because it is the teaching in perfect correspondence with the times and the capacities of beings, thus making it the Way that all Buddhas support and protect.

Unfortunately, the karma of those who slander the Nembutsu teaching, by denying the very existence of Amida Buddha and His Pure Land is so evil that they will be reborn in the Avici hell where they stay for a time impossible to calculate with our limited minds. People like them *"seem blind by nature and have no intrinsic goodness"* which also means that they do not have *"good from the past"*, as Rennyo Shonin explained. The good from the past represents our good karma from past lives and this life (prior to the awakening of faith) which manifests itself as an opening or receptive state of mind towards the message of the Primal Vow of Amida Buddha.

In deep harmony with His Master Honen, Shinran Shonin gave us an advice on how to treat those who slander the Nembutsu teaching both from the outside or inside of our school:

"Suppose that all other schools joined together in declaring, 'The Nembutsu is for the sake of worthless

people; that teaching is shallow and vulgar.' Even then, without the slightest argument, one should reply 'When foolish beings of inferior capacity like ourselves, persons ignorant of even a single letter, entrust themselves to the Vow, they are saved. Since we accept and entrust ourselves to this teaching, for us it is the supreme Dharma, though for those of superior capacity it might seem utterly base. Even though other teachings may be excellent, since they are beyond our capacity, they are difficult for us to put into practice. The fundamental intent of the Buddhas is nothing but freedom from birth-and-death for all, ourselves and others included, so you should not obstruct our practice of the Nembutsu.' If one responds without rancor thus, what person will do one harm? Moreover, there is an authoritative passage that states, 'Where disputation takes place, blind passions arise. The wise keep their distance.'

Shakyamuni taught that there would be both people who entrust themselves to this teaching and people who abuse it. By the fact that I have entrusted myself fully to it and there are others who abuse it, I realize that the Buddha's words are indeed true. Hence, I realize all the more clearly that my birth [in the Pure Land] is indeed firmly settled. If there were none who abused the teaching, then surely, we would wonder why there are those who entrust but none who abuse it. This is not to say the Nembutsu necessarily must be slandered; I merely speak of the fact that the Buddha, knowing beforehand that there would be both those who trust and those who slander, taught this so people would have no doubts."[38]

The words *"where disputation takes place, blind passions arise. The wise keep their distance"* are similar with Honen's, *"those who criticize and slander the teaching of Nembutsu are merely obsessed with illogical reasons, which are not worthy of debate."*

Our Path is not based on the flawed logic of the unenlightened minds but on the direct revelations and instructions of Shakyamuni about Amida Buddha in the *Larger Sutra*. It is a teaching that must be accepted in faith as He clearly instructed:

*"If there are sentient beings who have heard it, they will attain the stage of non-retrogression for realizing the highest Enlightenment. This is why you should single-heartedly **accept in faith**, uphold, and chant this sutra, and practice in accordance with its teachings."*

Insisting further on the importance of not having any doubt about the contents of this sutra, Shakyamuni said:

"'I have expounded this teaching for the sake of sentient beings and enabled you to see Amitayus (Amida) and all in His land. Strive to do what you should. After I have passed into Nirvana[39]*, do not allow doubt to arise."*[40]

---

[38] *Tannisho,*The Collected Works of Shinran, Shin Buddhism Translation Series, Jodo Shinshu Hongwanji-ha, Kyoto, 1997, p.669

[39] Passing into Nirvana, or to be more precise, into Parinirvana, is an expression used by the Buddha to refer to leaving the human

When having such a clear instruction from the World Honored One and the testimony of Ananda who literally saw Amida and His Pure Land, what is there to be debated?

---

body He manifested to teach in our human plane of existence. Actually, His mind has always dwelled in Nirvana or the state of perfect Enlightenment.

[40] The Three Pure Land Sutras - A Study and Translation from Chinese by Hisao Inagaki in collaboration with Harold Stewart, Bukkyo Dendo Kyokai and Numata Center for Buddhist Translation and Research, Kyoto, 2003, p.70

On people who cannot be saved by Amida

"Indeed, it matters not how vile we be whether in body or in mind. Whoever we are, we ought to put our trust in Amida's Vow, and bend our whole mind to the one way, and so we shall assuredly be born into the Pure Land. Nevertheless, we must remember that many men have many minds. There are some who look only for the pleasure and glory of this present evanescent world, which is but a vision or a dream, and know nothing at all about that afterworld. There are others again who have come to dread the future, and accordingly bend their energies in that direction. Thus, their minds flit from this to that religious practice, and they do not trust exclusively in the one and only way. Again, there are some who, when they have once made up their minds in a certain way, will not change them, but persist therein in spite of everything they may hear. Then there are others who today have a most excellent faith, and it would seem as if they could never deviate therefrom a hair's breadth, and yet they afterwards give it up entirely. Such being the case it is very hard to find anyone who has really entered the gate of Jodo (Pure Land), and is devoting himself heart and soul to the practice of the Nembutsu alone. I seem to myself to be the only one who secretly grieves over such a regrettable state of things, and indeed it is hard to find anyone in this world, who gives heed to the Dharma itself,

irrespective of the character of the man who expounds it."[41]

Commentary:
Amida Buddha wishes to save everybody. However, there are some people He cannot save because they themselves refuse His salvation. Master Honen described some of these people in the fragment above.

1. *"There are some who look only for the pleasure and glory of this present evanescent world, which is but a vision or a dream, and know nothing at all about that afterworld"*.
These are the atheists and materialists who believe that we have only one life and that nothing exists after death. Because they don't have any desire to escape samsara, they can't entrust to Amida Buddha or wish to be born in His Pure Land.

To our surprise, we find many of this category in religion too, and especially in Jodo Shinshu Buddhism! They are those scholars who treat the Buddha Dharma like a mere object of study, who dislike the devotional attitude of simple faith devotees, calling it folk religion, and who deny rebirth and the existence of Amida Buddha, while insisting that the Pure Land is in the mind and not an enlightened place to be attained after death. I would have no problem with these guys if they stick to

---

[41] Honen the Buddhist Saint - His Life and Teachings, volume III, compiled by imperial order, translation by Rev Ryugaku Ishizuka and Rev Harper Havelock Coates, The Society for the Publication of Sacred Books of the World, Kyoto, 1949, p. 412-413

their academic circles but they wear the robes and kesa of priests and teachers, doing ceremonies in front of temple altars, mimicking religion when they are actually nonreligious and even disregard the very basics of the Pure Land school - Amida Buddha himself. They bow in front of His image but do not actually accept His existence and they do funeral services without believing in life after death! I call this category of people - spiritual perverts. They are frustrated by their empty life as atheists and materialists and try to fill their inner nothingness through religious status. Theirs is the most disgusting way of life as what they do is spiritual thievery, dressing in the robes of a religion that they deny every time they open their mouth, doing worshipping gestures towards the images of Amida in whom they don't believe and chanting religious hymns whose content they don't follow. The need to be praised and respected as teachers is immense in such pitiful forms of life that they make so much efforts to be ordained and reach the highest status inside religious institutions. Truly for them, *"the pleasure and glory of this present evanescent world"* is all that matters. Not only that such people cannot be saved but they condemn themselves to the Avici hell for the evil act of slandering the right Dharma and shutting the door to liberation for others. These worms inside the lion's body[42] are worse than mass killers because they do not destroy bodies, but the medicine given by the Buddhas to liberate beings from birth and death. Their actions are like killing all

---

[42] People of wrong views are sometimes called "worms in the body of a lion". The lion here stands for the Dharma.

sentient beings again and again, ad infinitum. Ordinary people who don't believe in life after death or in transcendental Buddhas but stay out of religion and focus on their material welfare and glory, although they too cannot be saved by Amida, have an infinitely better karma than fake priests and teachers who pretend to speak in the name of Jodo Shinshu Buddhism while denying its basic doctrine and faith.

2. *"There are others again who have come to dread the future, and accordingly bend their energies in that direction. Thus, their minds flit from this to that religious practice, and they do not trust exclusively in the one and only way."*
These are people prone to superstition who are ready to do any practice that promises them safety. They are always scared of whatever may happen to them and so they lose the right perspective that samsara will never be safe anyway, and that the goal should be to escape it rather than trying to fix it. They are sometimes afraid to leave monotheistic religions and join Buddhism because they think that something bad might happen to them, like a punishment from their god. I met many people like this. Unfortunately, they are easily misguided by various nonbuddhist religions and cannot follow the *"one and only way"* which is the Primal Vow of Amida Buddha.

3. *"There are some who, when they have once made up their minds in a certain way, will not change them, but persist therein in spite of everything they may hear."*
These are people who will remain closed to the Primal Vow no matter how much we strive to explain it, or even

if they have in us true examples of faith in Amida. Many practitioners will not be able in this life to break away from the paradigm of self-power Buddhism. And they don't seem to hurry to escape birth and death, doing what they do in a relaxed way like they have all the time in the world. Some are also fixated in their preconceived opinions on the meaning of spirituality and religion, and the idea of Amida's help to attain Buddhahood quickly is impossible to understand and accept especially because it is too easy and simple.

4. *"There are others who today have a most excellent faith, and it would seem as if they could never deviate therefrom a hair's breadth, and yet they afterwards give it up entirely."*
Some people come to Jodo Shinshu and they seem to have faith but for some reason they cannot keep their shit together and constantly abandon it for other practices. Then they come back only to leave again after some months or a year. I have met so many in this category. They seem to have something like a mental or spiritual illness as they are mature people from whom one would expect some stability, but they simply cannot stay in one place (focused on one Path) for long time. Many people like this also have some kind of perverse wish to be in the front, speak publicly, and they even engage in organizing things in a sangha, making everyone have high expectations from them, until one day everything is over and they leave just like that, as if nothing happened. Believe me, I know people who do this coming and going for years and they never stop! They create chaos in every community they go and they too cannot be saved

by Amida because their instability proves that they don't have genuine faith (shinjin). Not all of them are that bad like people in the first category, but still they are very evil as they too are searching for status and public acceptance, talking about the Dharma when they should shut up, listen deeply and train their minds to be stable. It is important to stay away from them just like those in the first category.

Also, because the Pure Land Dharma is so simple and easy to understand (especially in the style we teach it at Amidaji) many people seem to have faith just because they understood it intellectually. Thus, we can easily confuse momentary enthusiasm with faith, which is another way to understand the above passage from Honen.

In our times as well as Honen's there is really hard to find people who dedicate themselves exclusively to the saying of the Nembutsu and who have true faith in Amida Buddha. Very few are really satisfied with the simple requirements of the Primal Vow and many feel the need to add something new or change the teaching so as to accommodate it to their personal opinions or various worldly ideologies.

There is another important element that Master Honen emphasized in this fragment: *"it is hard to find anyone in this world, who gives heed to the Dharma itself, irrespective of the character of the man who expounds it"*. This means that when hearing the Dharma, one should pay attention to the Dharma and not judge the teacher for things he does in his private life. Especially during this Last Dharma Age monks and nuns who act as teachers cannot be judged by the standards of the monks and nuns of the Right Dharma Age when Shakyamuni or His direct disciples were present in human form. I explained this (based on passages in the sutras) in chapter *Monks and nuns of the Last Dharma Age*, from my book *On the Monks and Nuns of Amidaji Branch of Jodo Shinshu Buddhism,* which is the doctrinal base for Amidaji ordination system. While no unenlightened being is perfect, the Amida Dharma which is taught and proclaimed by all the Enlightened Ones is perfect, so anyone who can clearly and faithfully transmit this Dharma is worthy of the respect of humans and gods. A wise person is able to distinguish between the personal blind passions of a teacher and the Dharma he or she transmits and will not shut his ears when hearing the truth, no matter how sinful is the voice who proclaims it. Namo Amida Bu

The meaning of "no working is true working" in relation with our birth in the Pure Land

Honen Shonin said:

"If you think that birth in the Pure Land is possible through your own efforts, you will become consumed with conceit that you are wise. When you possess this heart of conceit, you will not be in accord with the Primal Vow, and you will lose the protection of Amida Buddha as well as that of other Buddhas[43]. You are ultimately haunted by malevolent spirits. I here repeat - be vigilant indeed against conceit."[44]

Commentary:
Amida Buddha can protect us if we are totally connected to Him, that is, if we let go of any idea of improving our chances to be born in the Pure Land. We must always remember these golden words, "let go and let Amida". Let go of your tendency to play smart in samsara and let Him save you. We are not and we'll never be spiritual heroes, but only mere imitators, no matter whether we wear monk robes or the clothes of lay people. Only if we

---

[43] I explained the protection of Amida and other Buddhas as well as the protection offered by various deities to the person of faith in my book *The Meaning of Faith and Nembutsu in Jodo Shinshu Buddhism*, chapter on *The Ten Benefits in this Life*

[44] Honen Shonin, Instruction in the Seven Articles. *The Promise of Amida Buddha - Honen's Path to Bliss*; English translation of the Genko edition of the works of Honen Shonin - *Collected Teachings of Kurodani Shonin: The Japanese Anthology (Wago Toroku)*, translated by Joji Atone and Yoko Hayashi, Wisdom Publications, Boston, 2011, p.141

let go and let Amida can we be protected by Amida because any protection works within the law of cause and effect. If the cause of our practice is our unenlightened personalities, then the effect is that we are influenced by unenlightened forces and malevolent spirits who roam everywhere around us. If the cause of our practice is Amida Buddha, that is, if we rely completely on Him for our birth in the Pure Land, then the effect will automatically be related to Amida. Please bear in mind that He cannot protect those that do not rely on Him because the karmic cause for this protection is missing. This is a natural law, just like the moon cannot be reflected in a covered bowl of water or the rays of the sun cannot enter a room with closed windows.

Shinran Shonin also said in agreement with his Master, Honen:

"When people are not in correspondence with the Primal Vow,
Various conditions arise to trouble and confuse them.
To lose sight of shinjin (faith) in confusion
Is to 'lose right-mindedness'."[45]

He also said, quoting Honen:

"Know that shinjin (faith) is the true intent of the Pure Land teaching. When one has understood this, then as our teacher Master Honen declared, 'Other Power

---

[45] *The Collected Works of Shinran*, Shin Buddhism Translation Series, Jodo Shinshu Hongwanji-ha, Kyoto, 1997, p.381

means that no working is true working'. 'Working' [that is negated] is the calculating heart and mind of each practitioner. As long as one possesses a calculating mind, one endeavors in self-power. You must understand fully the working of self-power."[46]

Faith (shinjin) is the cause of birth in the Pure Land. This faith is in Amida alone, not in ourselves. Jodo Shinshu or the True Pure Land teaching of Master Honen and Shinran does not say "trust yourself" or "be your own light". Just as light is not produced by the walls of a room but by an exterior power source, so we are saved not by our own limited power but by Amida's hand that is extended to us.

Jodo Shinshu does not deny that we can be successful in our professional or personal life. However, being a good engineer, doctor, husband, wife, etc., is not the same as being a Buddha. Becoming a Buddha through our self-power is like trying to reach the Moon with a bicycle. So, discussions on self-power vs Other Power (Amida's Power) are held only in relation to birth in the Pure Land and the attainment of Buddhahood. Only in this matter do our calculations and mind categories not apply. We can design a good car or a sophisticated engine, but we cannot design our birth in the Pure Land:

"Other Power means that no working is true working. 'Working [that is negated] is the practitioner's

---

[46] Shinran Shonin, Notes on the Inscriptions on Sacred Scrolls, *The Collected Works of Shinran*, Shin Buddhism Translation Series, Jodo Shinshu Hongwanji-ha, Kyoto, 1997, p.520

calculating and designing. Tathagata's Primal Vow surpasses conceptual understanding; it is a design of the wisdom of Buddhas. It is not the design of foolish beings. No one can fathom the wisdom of Buddhas, which surpasses conceptual understanding. [...] Thus, the great teacher Honen said, 'No working is true working'. My understanding has been that nothing apart from this realization is necessary for the attainment of birth into the Pure Land; therefore, what others may say is of no concern to me."[47]

We are like ignorant peasants who know nothing about flying technology, yet still they trust the pilot and jump on the board of a plane to be taken to their desired destination. We do not know the exact technical supernatural details of how the Primal Vow works but we know it works, so we simply let Amida take us to His Pure Land.

By abandoning any tendency to try to work our minds to attain birth in the Pure Land *("not working")* Amida can do His saving work on us *("true working")*.
Namo Amida Bu

---

[47] Shinran Shonin, Lamp for the Latter-Ages, letter 7, *The Collected Works of Shinran*, Shin Buddhism Translation Series, Jodo Shinshu Hongwanji-ha, Kyoto, 1997, p.533

The protection by Amida Buddha can reach only those who exclusively say His Name in faith

" The merit of protection by Amida Buddha is received in daily life. This is because one who has genuine belief in birth in the Pure Land holds no doubt. Amida Buddha casts eighty-four thousand rays of His light of compassion upon one who is resolute in the attainment of this goal. Amida Buddha shines this light continually on the Nembutsu practitioner in daily life and up to the final moment of that person's life. For this reason, it is called the 'Vow by which Amida Buddha never abandons the Nembutsu devotee.'"[48]

When saying the above, Honen Shonin relied on the following passage from the *Contemplation Sutra*:

*"Buddha Amitayus (Amida) possesses eighty-four thousand physical characteristics, each having eighty-four thousand secondary marks of excellence. Each secondary mark emits **eighty-four thousand rays of light**; each ray of light shines universally upon the lands of the ten directions, embracing and not forsaking those who are mindful of the Buddha (have faith in Amida)."*[49]

---

[48] Honen Shonin, Essential Discourse on Birth in the Pure Land through Nembutsu.*The Promise of Amida Buddha - Honen's Path to Bliss*; English translation of the Genko edition of the works of Honen Shonin - *Collected Teachings of Kurodani Shonin: The Japanese Anthology (Wago Toroku)*, translated by Joji Atone and Yoko Hayashi, Wisdom Publications, Boston, 2011, p.126

[49] The Three Pure Land Sutras - A Study and Translation from Chinese by Hisao Inagaki in collaboration with Harold Stewart,

And he was also in complete agreement with Master Shan-tao:

"There are sentient beings who solely think on Amida Buddha; only these people are constantly illumined by the Light of that Buddha's heart, grasped and protected, never to be abandoned. It is not at all stated that any practitioner of various other acts (practices) is illumined and embraced. This is being protected in the present life, a manifestation of the decisive cause of birth in the Pure Land".[50]

Any Dharma method related with a specific Buddha assures some kind of protection if it's done correctly, but here we speak only about the protection of those who rely exclusively on Amida Buddha's Primal Vow. It is not like Amida wishes to arbitrarily save some while rejecting others, or that He saves only those who please Him. As I explained in the previous chapter, Amida's work of salvation takes place within the law of cause and effect, so He actually cannot save or illuminate those who refuse His salvation. It is like the light of the sun who spreads everywhere cannot illuminate the rooms with closed windows.

Bukkyo Dendo Kyokai and Numata Center for Buddhist Translation and Research, Kyoto, 2003, p. 87

[50] Shinran Shonin quoted that passage from Shan-tao's *Methods of Contemplation on Amida Buddha* in his Notes on Once-calling and Many-calling. *The Collected Works of Shinran*, Shin Buddhism Translation Series, Jodo Shinshu Hongwanji-ha, Kyoto, 1997, p.478

Shinran Shonin also said, in agreement with Master Honen and Master Shan-tao:

*"Countless Amida Buddhas reside
In the Light of the Buddha of Unhindered Light;
Each one of these transformed Buddhas protects
The person of true and real shinjin (faith)".*[51]

The countless transformed Amida Buddhas manifested in His Light are various Nirmanakayas or adaptation bodies of Amida who are always present with the person of faith. Amida Buddha is beyond any form in His Dharmakaya (absolute/ultimate) aspect, dwells with His transcendent form (Sambhogakaya) in the Pure Land, and in the same time He is here with us, people who have genuine faith in Him, in His various Accommodated and Transformation Bodies (Nirmanakayas). Wherever we are, in our room, on the street, alone or with friends and family, Amida Buddha is always accompanying us and illuminates us if we exclusively entrust to Him and say His Name in faith.

Shakyamuni assured us of Amida's extraordinary capacities:

"Amitayus (Amida), exercising supernatural powers at

---

[51] Shinran Shonin, Hymns of the Pure Land (Jodo Wasan) - Hymns of the Benefits in the Present, The Collected Works of Shinran, Shin Buddhism Translation Series, Jodo Shinshu Hongwanji-ha, Kyoto, 1997, p.355

will, can freely manifest His various forms in the lands of the ten directions"[52]

Exclusivity is extremely important if we want to benefit from the protection of Amida's Light. Again, because everything is cause and effect, we can be saved and protected by Amida only if we come in karmic agreement with His Primal Vow, where the causes of birth in His Pure Land are mentioned: exclusive faith in Him, exclusive saying of His Name and exclusive wish to be born in His Pure Land. This means, no other faith, no other practices and no other aspiration should enter the heart and mind of an Amida devotee. For the light of the sun to completely illuminate your room, you must open all your windows, not just one. In the same way, for Amida Buddha to protect and save you, all focus should be on Him alone. If you are hurt and somebody carries you on his back to safety, you must let yourself into his power and not hinder his movements by grabbing various trees and obstacles on the way. If you want Amida to save you and protect you, then let yourself into His Power and do not hinder him by changing your focus on other practices and teachings not related with His Primal Vow.

---

[52] Contemplation Sutra, The Three Pure Land Sutras - A Study and Translation from Chinese by Hisao Inagaki in collaboration with Harold Stewart, Bukkyo Dendo Kyokai and Numata Center for Buddhist Translation and Research, Kyoto, 2003, p.91

There is no need to wait for the coming of Maitreya Buddha when Amida's Primal Vow is available here and now

"Ajari[53] Koen, the abbot of the Kudokuin Temple, and one of Honen's teachers hailing from the province of Higo, was a noted scholar who was learned in the doctrines of both the esoteric and exoteric sects, and himself a disciple of Hokkyo Kokaku of Sugyu on Mount Hiei. One day as he was reflecting seriously upon life, and considering the limitations of his own powers, he thought that it would be no easy thing for him to get free from the fated round of life and death, and that every time he would change his state of existence, he would, as the doctrine goes, forget what had happened to him in the one before, and so, he thought, he would probably in the next life forget what he had now learned about the Teaching of the Buddhas. 'I have', he said, 'indeed been born a man, but I am so unfortunate as to have come into the world in the period between the appearance of the two Buddhas, and so I see nothing for it but that I must go through transmigration after transmigration. But in order to be able to meet the Merciful One (Maitreya) when He finally appears in the world, I should like to have my body changed into that of some being that has long life. So, there is nothing better for me

---

[53] Ajari (阿闍梨) is a Japanese term that is used in various schools of Buddhism in Japan, specifically Tendai and Shingon, in reference to a senior monk who teaches students; often abbreviated to jari. The term is a Japanese rendering of the Chinese transliteration for the Sanskrit "âcârya," one who knows and teaches the rules. (Wikipedia)

than to be born a serpent. I therefore vow that I shall be born a great serpent (naga). Only there is one thing I am afraid of, and that is the mighty gold-winged bird (Garuda)[54] that lives on the serpents dwelling in the great sea. My wish therefore is to live in a pond.' So, he made a bargain for a pond called Sakura-ga-ike[55] in the village of Kasawara in the province of Totomi, receiving the deed of it from its owner. When he came to die, he asked for some water which he put in the palm of his hand and then passed away.

On a certain day sometime afterwards, although there had been neither rain nor wind, the water in the pond, to the astonishment of everybody, kept increasing in volume, till there were such big waves that all the filth of the pond was washed away. When this was told to the

---

[54] Garuda are the natural enemies of nagas.

[55] Sakura-ga-ike at Kasahara – a small pond situated at a spot SE of Ike-shinden, Ogasa county, Totomi, about 13 English miles S of Horinouchi on the Tokaido railway. This pond is surrounded by mountains on three sides – north, east and west. On the northern side stands the Ike shrine, which is dedicated to the god of the pond. A curious festival is held in the autumn equinox every year, in which many rice-tubs full of sekihan (rice boiled with red beans) are carried by good swimmers to the center of the pond, and pushed down into the water, so as to be accepted by the god as offerings made to him. The county of Kasahara in Honen's day is said to have been the domain of Tadamasa Kwazan-in. It is said that Honen visited the pond for the rescue of his teacher Koen, who died in 1169, six years before Honen founded the new way of salvation. Koen is believed to have turned into a serpent and is still living in this pond. The Osho-kyo-in temple at Nakauchida in commemoration of Honen's visit, transferred its allegiance from the Tendai to the Jodo sect. (Footnote to the text at page 546.)

man who had previously owned it, he remembered that the day the waters became so swollen was the very day on which the Ajari died. It is said that to this very day, on a still night, you can hear the sound of a sacred bell ringing at the bottom of the pond. Surely it is very remarkable that such an event should happen in these latter days.

Honen on hearing this story, remarked, 'He was indeed a wise man, and well knew the difficulty of getting release from the round of transmigration, and so with a truly religious mind, he longed to meet the All-Merciful One (Maitreya). But the wish he realized of being born such a loathsome creature as a serpent was entirely due to his ignorance of the principles of the Pure Land doctrine. If I had only known this myself before the Ajari died, I should certainly have told him, whether he believed me or not. The fact is that after a man has attained birth in the Land of Perfect Bliss, he is free to go at pleasure anywhere in any of the ten directions of the universe, and so he can meet any or all of the Buddhas he wishes, and offer his devotion to them. What need is there, then, for him to go on living so long in this corrupt world? What a pity then for the Ajari to be wasting his time living in a pond waiting for the coming of the great Buddha of the future (Maitreya)!' "[56]

---

[56] Honen the Buddhist Saint - His Life and Teachings, volume III, compiled by imperial order, translation by Rev Ryugaku Ishizuka and Rev Harper Havelock Coates, The Society for the Publication of Sacred Books of the World, Kyoto, 1949, p. 535-536

Commentary:
As far as I understood, Ajari Koen made the aspiration to be reborn as a naga. According to the sacred texts, nagas are animals with miraculous powers who live in many places: in some realms of the gods or humans, below the four continents or in depths of waters (oceans, rivers, lakes, etc) where they have their own parallel reality, invisible to us, with cities, palaces and various manifestations. The nagas have many similarities with the spirits and have miraculous powers but are included in the category of animals because of their body in the form of big hooded snakes like cobras, and also probably because of their powerful animal instincts[57]. To be reborn as such a creature has some advantages like living a long life and having the capacity to become invisible and shapeshift (the sacred texts often mention them to appear in human form, although they can take other forms, too) and disadvantages like being killed and eaten by garudas[58] who are their natural enemies.

---

[57] You can read more explanations about nagas in the section dealing with animals from my book *The Four Profound Thoughts Which Turn the Mind Towards Amida Dharma*.

[58] Garudas, the second type of animals with miraculous powers, are very big birds with incredible strength, being capable of pulling up banyan trees from their roots (Jataka, 412, 543) or creating a powerful wind with the flapping of their wings (Jataka, 518) through which they separate the waters of the ocean and find nagas dwelling places (Jataka, 412) or causing a storm which can destroy human houses and plunge a whole town into total darkness (Jataka, 360). Also, because of their supranatural powers, garudas can shapeshift, often taking human form. You can read more explanations about garudas in the section related to animals in my book *The Four Profound Thoughts Which Turn the Mind Towards Amida Dharma*.

Maitreya[59] is, as you know, the future Buddha that will take up the role and activity of Shakyamuni. Ajari Koen lamented that although he was born a human being, he was living in a period between the two Buddhas, Shakyamuni and Maitreya. It is indeed beneficial to practice the Dharma under the personal guidance of a Buddha in physical form but this does not justify his later decision. Unfortunately, despite his devotion to the Dharma he did not have the karmic openness towards Amida Buddha, as I am sure Ajari Koen heard about the Pure Land teaching but perhaps he misunderstood it or dismissed it as being too easy to be true.

The idea of transferring the merits of one's practices and good deeds towards rebirth in the era when Maitreya appears in our world is common to many followers. Although there is nothing wrong with having devotion towards Him, it is definitely useless and not practical to aspire to remain in samsara until His appearance in our world, when we can simply entrust to Amida and join the stage of those assured of birth in the Pure Land. Some people will indeed be born at that time due to various causes and conditions but that doesn't mean that you, the reader of these lines, should make that aspiration when Amida Buddha is already available here and now.
If you are in a house on fire you should accept to be saved by the first fireman who comes at the scene and do not wait for the second. Similarly, one should accept Amida's helping hand that takes him to liberation soon,

---

[59] Miroku in Japanese.

rather than waiting for Maitreya who will come in a very distant future. Who knows what will happen to you until Maitreya comes? Even though your aspiration might be strong now you can always retrogress and lose whatever merits you think you accumulated and although you will be born during Maitreya's time you might be an insect without the capacity to understand His Dharma. Many things can happen during the long time between your present life and Maitreya's coming! Even if you are a long living snake (naga) your mind can become obscured and reach a point when you become uninterested in the Buddha Dharma, so Maitreya's coming might catch you unprepared, or you can die from various illnesses. There is absolutely NO guarantee that one's life or one's many lives will be a straight line towards the era of Maitreya, but there is a CERTAINTY that Amida Buddha will save you if you entrust to Him and say His Name during your present life. This is why Ajari Koen's decision was plainly stupid.

Even if we are now between the periods of the two Buddhas (Shakyamuni and Maitreya), we also live in the never-ending time of Amida who is constantly available in any era for those who wish to quickly escape birth and death.

Also, what do some practitioners think that Maitreya will teach? Actually, His main reason for the appearance in the world will be the same as that of Shakyamuni – to promote the Primal Vow of Amida. This happens with all Buddhas from countless universes as their main objective is to transmit the Amida Dharma. Already in the *Larger Sutra* we saw that Shakyamuni Buddha entrusted the teaching on Amida to Maitreya who was an active listener and interlocutor together with Ananda[60]:

"Now you have encountered a Buddha, listened to His expositions of the Dharma, and been able to learn about Amitayus (Amida). What pleasure and joy this is for you and me to share!
I share the joy with you."[61]

This means, I chose you *("you have encountered a Buddha")* for the transmission of this Dharma about Amida – *"what pleasure and joy this is for you and me to share! I share the joy with you"*.

Maitreya asked all the questions in the *Larger Sutra* for our sake (not because He did not know the answers) and He always received with devotion what Shakyamuni taught:

"Bodhisattva Maitreya prostrated himself on the ground and said, 'Your majestic glory, O Buddha, is awe-inspiring, and your exposition is most pleasing to me. Having heard your teaching I feel deeply that people of

---

[60] Read my book *Commentary on the Sutra on the Buddha of Infinite Life (Larger Sutra)*, pages 455-458 and all other references to Maitreya from that sutra.

[61] *The Three Pure Land Sutras - A Study and Translation from Chinese* by Hisao Inagaki in collaboration with Harold Stewart, Bukkyo Dendo Kyokai and Numata Center for Buddhist Translation and Research, Kyoto, 2003, p.52

the world are just as you have described"[62], that is, without any true capacity to liberate themselves from samsara through their own efforts.

"Your compassionate revelation of the Great Way has opened our eyes and ears, awakening us to liberation. Those who have heard your teachings are all filled with joy. Devas, humans, and lesser beings, including even those that crawl, have all been blessed by your compassionate guidance and have thereby attained deliverance from suffering and affliction".[63]

He is also recorded as saying:

"Maitreya said to the Buddha, 'Having received your considerate admonition, we will diligently practice the Way and follow your teaching. We will not allow any doubt to arise.'"[64]

So, as Maitreya himself accepted the teaching of Shakyamuni about Amida Buddha and because He will

---

[62] *The Three Pure Land Sutras - A Study and Translation from Chinese* by Hisao Inagaki in collaboration with Harold Stewart, Bukkyo Dendo Kyokai and Numata Center for Buddhist Translation and Research, Kyoto, 2003, p.51

[63] *The Three Pure Land Sutras - A Study and Translation from Chinese* by Hisao Inagaki in collaboration with Harold Stewart, Bukkyo Dendo Kyokai and Numata Center for Buddhist Translation and Research, Kyoto, 2003, p.51

[64] *The Three Pure Land Sutras - A Study and Translation from Chinese* by Hisao Inagaki in collaboration with Harold Stewart, Bukkyo Dendo Kyokai and Numata Center for Buddhist Translation and Research, Kyoto, 2003, p.53

transmit the same message when He appears in this world, why not entrust ourselves to Amida here and now? Why not follow His teaching and fulfill His heart desire? Shinran Shonin said:

*"Looking into the essence of the teachings of the Buddhas, we find that the true and fundamental intent for which **all the Tathagatas, past, present, and future**, appear in this world, is solely to teach the inconceivable Vow of Amida".*[65]

Thus, the best way to express your devotion and affinity with Maitreya is to say the Nembutsu of faith in Amida and reach His Pure Land after death.

At the end of our fragment Honen was recorded as saying:

"After a man has attained birth in the Land of Perfect Bliss, he is free to go at pleasure anywhere in any of the ten directions of the universe, and so he can meet any or all of the Buddhas he wishes, and offer his devotion to them[66]*".*

---

[65] *The Collected Works of Shinran*, Passages on the Pure Land Way, Shin Buddhism Translation Series, Jodo Shinshu Hongwanji-ha, Kyoto, 1997, p.317

[66] Just like in our world pupils who became themselves teachers often visit their former teachers to show their respect and gratitude, after we attain Buddhahood in the Pure Land, we will also visit our former teacher Buddhas and can even assist them in their activity to save sentient beings in their respective universes.

On what authoritative passages Honen Shonin relied when making such a statement? On some of the vows made by Amida Buddha himself and recorded by Shakyamuni in the *Larger Sutra*:

"If, when I attain Buddhahood, Bodhisattvas in my land[67] who would make offerings to Buddhas through my divine power, should not be able to reach immeasurable and innumerable kotis of nayutas of Buddha-lands in as short a time as it takes to eat a meal, may I not attain perfect Enlightenment."[68] (23rd Vow)

The passage showing the fulfilment of the 23rd Vow is in section 28 of the *Larger Sutra*, where Shakyamuni said:

"By the Buddha's power, Bodhisattvas of that land go to innumerable worlds of the ten directions, in as short a time as it takes to eat a meal, in order to pay homage and make offerings to the Buddhas and World-Honoured Ones."[69]

---

[67] The term "Bodhisattvas in my land" refer to Enlightened Bodhisattvas. I argued in the chapter dedicated to section 2 of my *Commentary on the Sutra on the Buddha of Infinite Life* and on my explanations of the 22nd vow from the same book that enlightened Bodhisattvas are actually Buddhas who manifest as Bodhisattvas. Please read that carefully.

[68] *The Three Pure Land sutras*, translated into English by Hisao Inagaki in collaboration with Harold Stewart, revised second edition, BDK English Tripitaka12-II, II, IV, Numata Center for Buddhist translation and Research, 2003, p.17

[69] *The Three Pure Land sutras*, translated into English by Hisao Inagaki in collaboration with Harold Stewart, revised second

The 24th Vow promises:

"If, when I attain Buddhahood, Bodhisattvas in my land should not be able, as they wish, to perform meritorious acts of worshipping the Buddhas with the offerings of their choice, may I not attain perfect Enlightenment.[70]

The passage showing the fulfilment of the 24th Vow is also in section 28 of the *Larger Sutra* where Shakyamuni said:

"If those Bodhisattvas so wish, countless and innumerable offerings, such as flowers, incense, music, silken canopies, and banners, spontaneously appear before them as soon as they are imagined. They are, accordingly, offered to the assemblies of Buddhas, Bodhisattvas, and Sravakas[71]*".*[72]

So, as you see from the above passages, there is absolutely no spiritual reason to remain in samsara and wait for Maitreya's coming:

---

edition, BDK English Tripitaka12-II, II, IV, Numata Center for Buddhist translation and Research, 2003, p.42

[70] *The Three Pure Land sutras*, translated into English by Hisao Inagaki in collaboration with Harold Stewart, revised second edition, BDK English Tripitaka12-II, II, IV, Numata Center for Buddhist translation and Research, 2003, p.17

[71] They are offered to Buddhas ruling those lands and to their Enlightened Assembly of Bodhisattvas and Sravakas (disciples).

[72] *The Three Pure Land sutras*, translated into English by Hisao Inagaki in collaboration with Harold Stewart, revised second edition, BDK English Tripitaka12-II, II, IV, Numata Center for Buddhist translation and Research, 2003, p.42

"What need is there, then, for him to go on living so long in this corrupt world? What a pity then for the Ajari to be wasting his time living in a pond waiting for the coming of the great Buddha of the future (Maitreya)!'"

Unfortunately, those who do not listen to Shakyamuni's teaching on Amida might also not listen to Maitreya's teaching on Amida when He will come to this world, and will probably not listen 1000 or 2000 years after His passing, aspiring to be born when the next Buddha after Maitreya comes, then the next one, and so on ad infinitum until for such people samsara will have no end. Please do not be like them.

Namo Amida Bu

The determination of the true disciple of Amida Buddha

Honen Shonin said:

"When a deer is being pursued by the hunters, it does not stop even to look around for its fellows or look back at its pursuers, but with all eagerness, hastens straight forward, and no matter how many may be following, it escapes in safety. It is with the same determination that a man fully entrusts himself to the Buddha's power, and without regard to anything else, steadfastly sets his mind upon being born into the Pure Land."[73]

Commentary:
A genuine disciple of Amida Buddha does not care about other practices and does not listen to the wrong views of modernists or the false teachings of externalists (non-Buddhists). Even if thoughts of "what if Amida is not real" or "what if the Primal Vow is not true" appear suddenly in his mind, he does not pay attention to them, but continues to be focused on the Nembutsu of faith. Instead of looking at these *"pursuers"* who come in the form of nonbuddhists, heretics or even random thoughts, he goes forward to the Pure Land encouraged by Shakyamuni and the lineage Masters.

---

[73] Honen the Buddhist Saint - His Life and Teachings, volume III, compiled by imperial order, translation by Rev Ryugaku Ishizuka and Rev Harper Havelock Coates, The Society for the Publication of Sacred Books of the World, Kyoto, 1949, p. 399

To be satisfied with the Nembutsu and to think that Nembutsu is enough, to not need anything else than Amida's Holy Name – these are the characteristics of a person of faith. Promises of other practices and religions fall on deaf ears because he obeys only the exclusive requirements of the Primal Vow: exclusive faith in Amida, exclusive saying of His Name and exclusive wish to be born in His Pure Land.

Even if the people around him follow other paths, or the stones and rocks, the sky and the trees all shout in one voice that Amida does not exist or that so and so God has a better teaching, the true disciple will never falter in his determination to have faith only in Amida, say only His Name and wish to go only to His Pure Land after death. Just like the deer pursued by hunters, he sees nothing, hears nothing and is not interested in any other path than the Nembutsu of faith. Only such a true disciple will reach the safety of the Pure Land.

Honen Shonin's letter to Shōnyobō

A nun called Shōnyobō who practiced Nembutsu and embraced the teaching of Honen Shonin became sick, and as she was lying on her death bed, she sent word that she would like to see him one last time. At that moment Honen was in a Nembutsu retreat and he wrote her the following letter (words in brackets are my own):

"I am very sorry indeed to hear about Shonyobo's illness. Having heard that she is ill, in fact seriously so, I should like to go and see her, and make sure whether she is going right on with the practice of the Nembutsu up to the very end; but especially so when I remember how often she used to call upon me to ask questions about the way of salvation. So as soon as word reached me, I at once wanted to go and see her. But I had just before that decided upon the special Nembutsu practice (Nembutsu retreat) for some days, and not to go out of my chamber for anything whatsoever. Now circumstances have so changed, that I am tempted to reverse my decision and go at once to see her. But on further reflection I have come to feel that, after all, it does not matter one way or the other about such interchanges of courtesy in this world, for the fact is that we are in danger anyway of becoming foolishly attached to these earthly bodies of ours. No matter who it is, no one stays forever here in this fleshly body. The only difference is that either I myself or someone else must be left behind and the other go first. Then if we think of the interval of time that will separate us, that too is uncertain. And even though they may call it long, at the longest it is only like a short

dream. So, no matter how many times I think it over, the more I am convinced that the thing to do is to think only of our meeting in the land of Amida Buddha where, as we sit upon our lotus flowers, the cares of this world will have all clear away, and we shall converse together about the scenes and events of our past lives.
We shall then take counsel together as to how we may help each other in promoting the salvation of human beings down through the long future. This is the same as I have always told her from the beginning, that she should take firm hold upon the Buddha's Primal Vow, not allowing one thought of doubt to enter her heart. And even though she can only repeat the Nembutsu but once, to remember that, however sinful she feels herself to be, she shall, by the power of the Buddha's Vow, without question be born into the Pure Land. So, tell her to apply herself with undivided mind to the repetition of the sacred Name.

Our birth into the Pure Land is not in the least related to our goodness, or badness, but solely depends upon Amida Buddha's Power. It matters not how high one's rank may be; in these latter evil days, birth into the Pure Land by one's own power is extremely difficult. As it is all by the Buddha's power, however sinful, foolish or unclean we may be, everything hangs solely upon our trusting in the Power of His Primal Vow.... There are indeed, I am very sorry to say, those who persist in saying that it is quite impossible to attain birth into the Pure Land. But however learned or noble in rank such persons may be, tell her not to pay any attention to what they say. They may indeed be excellent in their own way

*of thinking, but they have not yet reached
Enlightenment; and so, we may say that the words of
people who are trying to save themselves by their own
efforts are very great hindrances to those seeking Ojo
(birth into the Pure Land). Let us not therefore adopt the
methods of the unenlightened, but entrust ourselves to
the Buddha's Vow and that only. The good father Zendo
(Shantao) used to say, that we should not tolerate a
single thought of doubt, on account of the opposition
offered by those of another religious school to the Pure
Land doctrine ...*

*It is better not to call in people of a different faith, but
whoever they are, whether nuns or other ladies, tell her
to have them always at her side repeating the Nembutsu.
She should with one heart and mind lay aside all the
religious counsel of the unenlightened, and trust only in
the wise counsel of the Buddha ...*

*The fact is that in my own case, the decision I made to
shut myself up in my chamber for the Nembutsu practice
is by no means intended for myself alone. And since I
have heard of her illness, I shall direct all my prayers
without exception toward the one object of promoting
her birth in the Pure Land. So, tell her that I am praying
for her that her deepest desire for birth in the Pure Land
be fulfilled. How can it be otherwise than that this will
be helpful to her, if indeed my own purpose in it be
genuine? Believe me, it will certainly be effective. That
she has listened with such attention to my words, shows
a karma relationship extending beyond the limits of the
present world, and is deeply rooted in a pre-existent*

state. Now from what I hear, whether she precedes me into the other world or I unexpectedly precede her, there is no doubt whatever that we shall meet again at last in the same Pure Buddha land. It matters not whether we meet again in this world, which is but a fleeting dream. So let her not worry about that at all, but lay aside all such thoughts, and give every attention to the deepening and strengthening of her faith, and to the practice of the Nembutsu, and wait for the time when we shall meet in that Land ... If she is now very weak, I am afraid that what I have said may be too long for her to take in fully, and in that case, please just tell her the substance of what I have written. The news of her illness has stirred within me a strange sense of sorrow, which has impelled me to write".

They say that she kept thinking of this letter as she went on repeating the Nembutsu up to the very last, till her longing for birth in the Pure Land was finally realized."[74]

Commentary:
Master Honen was not acting without compassion for Shonyobo when he decided to not interrupt his Nembutsu retreat to see her for the last time. Any teacher needs a period of Dharma seclusion to recharge his spiritual batteries and focus on his mission with even

---

[74] Honen the Buddhist Saint - His Life and Teachings, volume III, compiled by imperial order, translation by Rev Ryugaku Ishizuka and Rev Harper Havelock Coates, The Society for the Publication of Sacred Books of the World, Kyoto, 1949, p. 375-378.

greater determination. Thus, his retreat was not an ego-centered activity, but a period of sitting alone with Amida Buddha in order to better help others: *"the decision I made to shut myself up in my chamber for the Nembutsu practice is by no means intended for myself alone"*. This is why he considered that personal attachment or courtesy is no good reason for meeting and interrupting his practice:

"But on further reflection I have come to feel that, after all, it does not matter one way or the other about such interchanges of courtesy in this world, for the fact is that we are in danger anyway of becoming foolishly attached to these earthly bodies of ours."

The samsaric time is an illusion, so even if one goes before us and we still remain in this world, when we finally meet in Sukhavati, we'll feel like we have always been there. Thus, instead of longing to see each other again in this samsaric dream out of attachment to their illusory faces, Honen advised her to focus on the goal of birth in the Pure Land where they will soon meet as Enlightened beings:

"It matters not whether we meet again in this world, which is but a fleeting dream. So let her not worry about that at all, but lay aside all such thoughts, and give every attention to the deepening and strengthening of her faith and to the practice of the Nembutsu, and wait for the time when we shall meet in that Land".

"Then if we think of the interval of time that will separate us, that too is uncertain. And even though they may call it long, at the longest it is only like a short dream. So, no matter how many times I think it over, the more I am convinced that the thing to do is to think only of our meeting in the land of Amida Buddha".

The final advice Honen gave to her was a wonderful presentation of the essential points of the true Pure Land teaching. Every one of us is on the death bed like Shonyobo as we can all die anytime, so we should take Honen's teaching to heart and entrust exclusively to Amida Buddha to secure our birth into the Pure Land. We must rely on Amida alone and don't think that our badness or so-called goodness can play any role in our salvation. We should understand that we are accepted as we are by Amida with all our uncleanliness and impurity of mind, just as Honen said:

"Our birth into the Pure Land is not in the least related to our goodness, or badness, but solely depends upon Amida Buddha's Power. It matters not how high one's rank may be; in these latter evil days, birth into the Pure Land by one's own power is extremely difficult. As it is all by the Buddha's power, however sinful, foolish or unclean we may be, everything hangs solely upon our trusting in the Power of His Primal Vow".

As for those who follow self-power practices and belong to other schools that do not believe in the Primal Vow, we should not take their sayings into consideration no matter how smart or spiritually advanced they think they are. Followers of the Pure Land Path should not mix various teachings and practices but rely on the requirements of the Primal Vow alone: exclusive faith in Amida, exclusive saying of His Name and exclusive wish to be born in His land. As Honen said:

"The words of people who are trying to save themselves by their own efforts are very great hindrances to those seeking Ojo (birth into the Pure Land)".

Thus, he advised Shonyobo and us, disciples of later times *"not to pay any attention to what they say."* More than this, such people who cling to their self-power are unenlightened while Amida who made the Primal Vow is perfectly Enlightened:

"Let us not therefore adopt the methods of the unenlightened, but entrust ourselves to the Buddha's Vow and that only. The good father Zendo (Shantao) used to say, that we should not tolerate a single thought of doubt, on account of the opposition offered by those of another religious school to the Pure Land doctrine"

When we have the most important guru and Master in the whole universe – Amida Buddha himself, why listen to the opinions of this or that unenlightened teacher who is obsessed with his own power and does not realize his own spiritual limitations? As long as Amida Buddha said – if you entrust to me, say my Name and wish to be born in my land, you will go there, then that is all we need. We should not let ourselves fall into doubts and confusion by the words of those who lack faith in the Primal Vow of Amida.

Shonyobo who was on her death bed and us who can die anytime should search for the company of those who say the Nembutsu of faith, and be deaf and blind to the words of unbelievers:

"It is better not to call in people of a different faith, but whoever they are, whether nuns or other ladies, tell her to have them always at her side repeating the Nembutsu. She should with one heart and mind lay aside all the religious counsel of the unenlightened, and trust only in the wise counsel of the Buddha".

The concept of prayer is introduced in this letter:

"I shall direct all my prayers without exception toward the one object of promoting her birth in the Pure Land. So, tell her that I am praying for her that her deepest desire for birth in the Pure Land be fulfilled".

Honen Shonin shows us that it is ok to pray for our dear ones to become open to Amida and be guided by Him. Of course, Amida Buddha is already doing His best and has been trying to save each and every being for eons, always having each one of us in front of His eyes constantly, but there is no doctrinal mistake if we pray for others and wish that they be free of obstacles and entrust to Amida. Shinran Shonin also mentioned prayer, this time in relation with those in error but of course, prayer can be used for everyone[75]:

"While holding the Nembutsu in your heart and saying it always, please pray for the present life and also the next life of those who slander it. [...] If you simply pray for the people in society who are in error and desire to lead them into Amida's Vow, it will be a response out of gratitude for the Buddha's benevolence".[76]

I think that Honen Shonin was convinced that Shonyobo had faith which is another reason that he did not feel there is a need to go personally to her death bed. He mentioned what Rennyo Shonin later called "good from the past" and the connection with a good teacher, which are two of the five conditions[77] for birth in the Pure Land:

"That she has listened with such attention to my words, shows a karma relationship extending beyond the limits

---

[75] Nembutsu itself is not a prayer but the expression of simple faith in Amida.

[76] Shinran Shonin, A Collection of Letters – letter 8, The Collected Works of Shinran, Shin Buddhism Translation Series, Jodo Shinshu Hongwanji-ha, Kyoto, 1997, p.570

[77] According to Master Rennyo , there are five conditions that someone must meet in order to be born in the Pure Land: 1) stored good from the past, 2) a good spiritual teacher, 3) Amida's light, 4) the entrusting heart (shinjin)
5) the saying of Amida Buddha's Name (Nembutsu). See my explanations in Fascicle 9 of *Amida Dharma* book.

of the present world, and is deeply rooted in a pre-existent state".

The "stored good from the past" represents our good karma from past lives and this life which manifests itself as an opening or receptive state of mind towards the message of the Primal Vow of Amida Buddha. A lot of people hear the teaching about the Primal Vow but few are opened to it. This openness is very important and is the manifestation of the good stored from the past. Also, if you listen again and again to the teaching in this life, thus becoming immersed with all your being in the Dharma, this listening will become a "stored good" which will make you open to the call of the Primal Vow.

Shonyobo was surely open to this Call and she already solved all her doubts by constantly asking Honen Shonin about the essentials of the teaching: *"I remember how often she used to call upon me to ask questions about the way of salvation".*

The final Dharma letter sent by her beloved teacher only added a final encouragement and a confirmation to what she already knew. Thus, she entered into the Pure Land while holding her teacher's last words in her heart and saying the Nembutsu of faith,

"They say that she kept thinking of this letter as she went on repeating the Nembutsu up to the very last, till her longing for birth in the Pure Land was finally realized".

We will meet Shonyobo in the Pure Land where she and other teachers or lay followers that went before us enjoy their Enlightenment and talk among themselves about how to help sentient beings entrust to Amida.

Namo Amida Bu

Goodness or badness are NOT the cause of birth into the Pure Land

"Some people were conversing about the future life, some saying that fish-eaters will be born in the Pure Land, others that they will not. Honen overhearing them said, 'If it is a case of eating fish, cormorants would be born into the Pure Land; and if it is a case of not eating them, monkeys would be so born. But I am sure that whether a man eats fish or not, if he only calls upon the sacred Name, he will be born into the Pure Land.'"[78]

Commentary:
There is a sentence in *Tannisho* which explains the reason for such useless discussions about eating or not eating meat in relation with birth in the Pure Land:

"In truth, myself and others discuss only good and evil, leaving Amida's benevolence out of consideration".[79]

It is important to understand that our salvation does not depend on something good we may find within ourselves, and that we are not obstructed in reaching the Pure Land because we are evil. As Shinran said:

---

[78] Honen the Buddhist Saint - His Life and Teachings, volume III, compiled by imperial order, translation by Rev Ryugaku Ishizuka and Rev Harper Havelock Coates, The Society for the Publication of Sacred Books of the World, Kyoto, 1949, p. 401

[79] The Collected Works of Shinran, Shin Buddhism Translation Series, Jodo Shinshu Hongwanji-ha, Kyoto, 1997, p.679

"For those who entrust themselves to the Primal Vow, no good acts are required, because no good surpasses the Nembutsu. Nor need they despair of the evil they commit, for no evil can obstruct the working of Amida's Primal Vow."[80]

If we compare the evil karma that is committed in all samsaric universes, and Amida's Name filled with infinite merits and virtues, it is like a tiny feather versus a sumo wrestler. Thus, we are not saved because we do this or that, eat meat or abstain from it, drink or not drink intoxicants, etc, but **because Amida Buddha loves us unconditionally.** By saying the Nembutsu of faith we enter into karmic connection with His love and salvific power.

To bring the notion of good or evil in matters related with our salvation is useless because these are NOT the cause for birth into the Pure Land (Ojo). If goodness was the cause of birth into the Pure Land, then only good people would go there. If badness was the cause of birth into the Pure Land, then only evil people would be born there. However, because the Pure Land is the creation/manifestation of Amida, it can be reached only through Amida, so when we say the Nembutsu of faith we abandon ourselves to His Power who will carry us safely to the Pure Land at the end of our samsaric bodies. It is also important to understand that Honen's answer was NOT an appeal to indulgence or a justification for

---

[80] *The Collected Works of Shinran*, Shin Buddhism Translation Series, Jodo Shinshu Hongwanji-ha, Kyoto, 1997, p.661

doing evil[81]. He had always advised people to do good deeds and improve their behavior in daily life. However, birth in the Pure Land is NOT related with good and evil but only with Amida's Power. Our good deeds or bad deeds are fuel for samsara (for birth into higher or lower states of existence), while the infinite supramundane merits of Amida invested in His Name are fuel for reaching the Pure Land. When we entrust for the first time in Amida, and we automatically say the Nembutsu of faith, we receive from Him the karmic energy for reaching His Pure Land.

Here are two more passages by Honen on the same topic. Please study them carefully:

"There is no need to reflect on virtue or vice, or to discuss the gravity of your negative karma. Establish an unshakable faith that if you simply mouth Namo Amida Butsu with the aspiration for birth in the Pure Land, you will most certainly attain birth in the Pure Land. **The karma of this birth will be determined by your degree of faith.** *Once you understand this, birth in the Pure Land*

---

[81] *"There seem to be many who say that behaving prudently and exerting efforts to become a good person in order not to commit unwholesome karma will demean the Primal Vow. Don't lend an ear to such misguided notions. In the first place,* **where in the holy text does Amida Buddha encourage you to commit an offense?"**
Honen Shonin, Instruction in the Seven Articles - *The Promise of Amida Buddha - Honen's Path to Bliss*; English translation of the Genko edition of the works of Honen Shonin - *Collected Teachings of Kurodani Shonin: The Japanese Anthology (Wago Toroku)*, translated by Joji Atone and Yoko Hayashi, Wisdom Publications, Boston, 2011, p.137

will be attained easily. The attainment of birth in the Pure Land will be uncertain only if you doubt this birth; the attainment of birth in the Pure Land will be certain if you believe in this birth. After all, **the profound faith is the firm belief without a shadow of doubt that the Primal Vow never abandons any person, regardless of the gravity of their karma**, *and that anyone will, with certainty, attain birth in the Pure Land with just a single utterance of the Name of Amida Buddha."*[82]

"Those who firmly believe in the definite attainment of birth in the Pure Land and repeat Namo Amida Butsu, Namo Amida Butsu - both the virtuous and the nonvirtuous, men and women, ten out of ten, or one hundred out of one hundred beings - will achieve birth in the Pure Land."[83]

---

[82] Honen Shonin, An Outline of the Doctrine for Birth in the Pure Land; *The Promise of Amida Buddha - Honen's Path to Bliss*; English translation of the Genko edition of the works of Honen Shonin - *Collected Teachings of Kurodani Shonin: The Japanese Anthology (Wago Toroku)*, translated by Joji Atone and Yoko Hayashi, Wisdom Publications, Boston, 2011, p.109

[83] Honen Shonin, Essential Discourse on Birth in the Pure Land through Nembutsu; *The Promise of Amida Buddha - Honen's Path to Bliss*; English translation of the Genko edition of the works of Honen Shonin - *Collected Teachings of Kurodani Shonin: The Japanese Anthology (Wago Toroku)*, translated by Joji Atone and Yoko Hayashi, Wisdom Publications, Boston, 2011, p.118 - 119

Nembutsu is the same no matter who says it

"When someone once said to Honen that his repetition of the Nembutsu must be very acceptable to the Buddha, he asked 'Why?'
'Because you are a wise man, and know in detail what merit there is in the repetition of the sacred Name, clearly understanding the meaning of the Buddha's Primal Vow.'
At this Honen replied: 'You have not yet really come to believe in the Primal Vow at all. As to calling upon the sacred Name of the Primal Vow of the Buddha Amida, it makes no difference whether the man be a wood-cutter, a gatherer of grass or greens, or a drawer of water or the like, whether he be utterly unlettered in Buddhism or other religions. It makes no difference, I say, so long as he calls upon the sacred Name. If he believes his Ojo (birth in the Pure Land) is certain and keeps repeating the Nembutsu, he is the very best kind of believer. If it is possible by wisdom to get free from the bondage of life and death, why indeed should I, Genku (Honen), have given up the Holy Path (Shodo-mon) and devoted myself exclusively to this Pure Land doctrine (Jodo-mon)? The self-discipline of the so-called Holy Path consists in the effort to escape birth and death by the cultivation of one's wisdom whereas that of the Pure Land consists in coming back to what the world calls foolishness, and thus attain birth into the Land of Bliss.'"[84]

---

[84] Honen the Buddhist Saint - His Life and Teachings, volume III, compiled by imperial order, translation by Rev Ryugaku Ishizuka and Rev Harper Havelock Coates, The Society for the Publication of Sacred Books of the World, Kyoto, 1949, p. 401

Commentary:
The only wisdom we can have on the Jodo Shinshu Path is to realize we are foolish people without a chance to escape samsara through our own power and that only Amida is able to lead us to perfect Enlightenment in His Pure Land.

Long time ago, there was a scholar who disagreed with my attempt to present the teaching about Amida in simple terms and he said that we should not make Jodo Shinshu look like it is only for idiots. "But we are all idiots", I said, "including you and me"! As long as we are not Buddhas yet, we are all idiots and foolish because only a Buddha has infinite wisdom and knows everything.
Although praised by many as very wise and knowledgeable in many sutras and treatises, Honen always considered himself a foolish person:

„I am nothing but the foolish Honen, weighed down by the ten evils, and I say that the only way for me to attain Ojo (birth in the Pure Land) is by calling upon the sacred Name."[85]

He also said:

---

[85] Honen the Buddhist Saint - His Life and Teachings, volume III, compiled by imperial order, translation by Rev Ryugaku Ishizuka and Rev Harper Havelock Coates, The Society for the Publication of Sacred Books of the World, Kyoto, 1949, p. 396-397

„An incapable man like me can only put His entire trust in the Great Vow".[86]

The reason why Nembutsu is the same no matter who says it, is because its effectiveness depends entirely on Amida's Power and not on something that can be found within ourselves.
If we could add anything to the holy Name of Amida or if we could improve it by our personal qualities, then it would matter who says it, but as the Name is filled with the myriad qualities of Amida, we should simply say it in faith without thinking of anything else.

---

[86] Honen the Buddhist Saint - His Life and Teachings, volume III, compiled by imperial order, translation by Rev Ryugaku Ishizuka and Rev Harper Havelock Coates, The Society for the Publication of Sacred Books of the World, Kyoto, 1949, p. 396

Focus on Amida's Name, not on your monkey mind

"Question: 'When evil thoughts will keep arising within the mind, what ought one to do?
Answer (by Honen Shonin): 'The only thing to do is to repeat the Nembutsu.'"[87]

Commentary:
This is something that I often say in my books, articles and discussions with my Dharma friends. We cannot fix our samsaric minds. We cannot eliminate evil thoughts. We cannot stop thinking. All we can to do is change the focus from whatever appears in our mind to Amida, through the saying of His Name. Just as you don't take a monkey serious, don't take your mind serious. We are not saved because of any so-called quality that can be found in our minds and we are not obstructed to be born in the Pure Land by our blind passions and evil thoughts. Our salvation comes from outside of our samsaric mind, so we do not need to bother about it anymore.

Accept yourself as you are because you are saved by Amida Buddha exactly as you are[88]. Accept that it is

---

[87] Honen the Buddhist Saint - His Life and Teachings, volume III, compiled by imperial order, translation by Rev Ryugaku Ishizuka and Rev Harper Havelock Coates, The Society for the Publication of Sacred Books of the World, Kyoto, 1949, p. 426

[88] Hoin Jogon, the chief priest of the Chikurimbo temple, asked Honen: *"What ought one to do when evil thoughts and passions come surging through his mind?"*. Honen answered: *"This is the working of the natural evil disposition of man, and the ordinary man is powerless to control it. But I am sure that deliverance and birth into the Pure Land may be obtained by wholly relying upon the*

impossible to have pure thoughts while you are still in this samsaric environment, itself the effect of personal and collective karma. Here everything is a temptation and an obstacle, so it's impossible that thoughts of attachments, desire, aversion, etc, do not arise in your mind. If you had no evil thoughts then you would be a Buddha, and for a Buddha the Primal Vow would be useless. In that Primal Vow Amida asked you to entrust to Him, say His Name and wish to be born in His Pure Land. He did not tell you to have pure thoughts or to develop special qualities in your mind. Basically, He asked you to come as you are, entrust to Him as you are with all your problems and blind passions, say His Name as you are, and wish to be born in His Pure Land as you are. There is no need to self-exclude yourself from His salvation by inventing obstacles that He never put in the Path to His Pure Land, so simply say His Name without worrying about your monkey mind.

There is no problem if your mind is agitated or chaotic. Nembutsu does NOT depend on your mind and is not improved or affected by anything that can be found in it. Why? Because the Name AMIDA belongs to AMIDA! You did not invent the Holy Name!

Primal Vow of Amida, by calling upon the sacred Name, and taking advantage of the power of the Buddha's Vow."
(Honen the Buddhist Saint - His Life and Teachings, volume II, compiled by imperial order, translation by Rev Ryugaku Ishizuka and Rev Harper Havelock) Coates, The Society for the Publication of Sacred Books of the World, Kyoto, 1949, p. 262-263

"Only Nembutsu is true and real", said Shinran Shonin, which means that Nembutsu does not belong to the illusory samsaric world, but to the reality of Enlightenment. I repeat this because it is extremely important - although we say it with our lips, Nembutsu does not belong to us and is not improved or affected by us. We can't soil Nembutsu with our thoughts. More than this, Nembutsu was invented especially for beings like us. It is not a mantra that should be recited in a special way or with a special state of mind, but a Name that can be easily said by anybody, no matter how high or low they are on the scale of spiritual evolution. It is the Name that does not exorcise demons, as demons themselves can say it in faith, be saved and transformed into Buddhas in the Pure Land of Amida. It is the Name that low level beings like us can say it as they are and enter the stage of non-retrogression for birth in the Pure Land. It is the ultimate expression of the Infinite Compassion of Amida and all Buddhas.

No matter where you go in the ten directions and no matter how far you search in all religions you cannot find a Name so powerful and yet so Compassionate and easily accessible to all.

Namo Amida Bu

Say Nembutsu as you are

Honen Shonin said, in reply to a question by Zenshobo:

"Those who think that it is only the Nembutsu of the pious and learned which can eventuate in Ojo (birth in the Pure Land), and that there is no Ojo for the ignorant and unlettered and those who go in sinning every day, even if they should say the Nembutsu, have not yet grasped the fact that the Primal Vow includes both the good and the bad.

It is impossible in this life to change man's nature, which he has inherited through the working of his karma from a pre-existent state, just in the same way as it is impossible for a woman in this life to be changed into a man, no matter how much she might desire it. Those who call upon the sacred Name should do it with the nature they now have, the wise man as a wise man, the fool as a fool, the pious as pious, the irreligious as irreligious, and thus all equally may attain Ojo.

Whether a man is rich and noble, or poor and mean, whether he is kind or unkind, avaricious or morose, indeed no matter what he is, if he only repeats the Nembutsu in dependence upon the mysterious power of the Primal Vow, his Ojo is certain. Amida's Primal Vow was made to take in all conceivable cases of people, whom He thus engaged to save, if they would but practice the Nembutsu. Without inquiring at all into the grade of their several capacities, but merely saying the

Nembutsu in their simple earnestness – this is all that is needed for anybody.

Bear in mind that everyone who thinks the Nembutsu Ojo is too lofty or too profound to be grasped has wholly mis-apprehended the very nature of the Primal Vow itself. Can it be that unless I, Genku (Honen), attain the highest rank as Betto or Kengyo[89], I cannot obtain Ojo, or that it would be quite beyond me if I remain merely what I was at my birth? Far from it. The fact is that all I have learned in my studies through the years is absolutely without avail in procuring me Ojo, and the one thing learning has taught me is its utter powerlessness to bring me Ojo."[90]

Commentary:
Buddha Dharma is not for Buddhas who are already Enlightened and free, but for those caught in illusion, blind passions and suffering. It is stupid to ask a Buddhist to behave like a Buddha, think like a Buddha or talk like a Buddha. Among all Dharma Gates, especially the Primal Vow of Amida takes us from where we are (unenlightened and sinful people), not from where we should be (enlightened and pure). It starts from the present, whatever that present is for various people, and it does not impose on us any special conditions on which to enter the Pure Land.

---

[89] I think these might be scholarly ranks.
[90] Honen the Buddhist Saint - His Life and Teachings, volume V, compiled by imperial order, translation by Rev Ryugaku Ishizuka and Rev Harper Havelock Coates, The Society for the Publication of Sacred Books of the World, Kyoto, 1949, p. 733-734

Faith in Amida, the saying of Amida's Name and the wish to be born in Amida's Land are effective because of Amida. Just as it is very important to have the right connections to obtain various worldly benefits, knowing and trusting Amida is the only Path to His Pure Land. In daily life the more powerful our connections are, the more chances we have to be successful, while in matters related with our Ojo, there is no better connection than the creator of the Land of Bliss – Amida Buddha himself. Thus, it is due to Amida that our Nembutsu recitation is effective in bringing us to Ojo. Because Amida put all His infinite merits, virtues and power in His Name, we enter the stage of non-retrogression for birth into His land in the exact moment we say the first Nembutsu of faith. I always choose my words carefully which is why I use the expression "Nembutsu of faith" as I want to make people aware that this is not the Nembutsu dependent on some special capacities that the reciter develops within oneself, but the Nembutsu of Amida centered Power. The disciple of the Primal Vow is focused on Amida and relies on Amida, not on his so-called good or bad qualities. This is why it does not matter who is the one saying the Nembutsu as long as he says it and entrusts to Amida.

Honen made reference in the above answer to Zenshobo to something that Shinran also explained in the thirteenth chapter of *Tannisho* – the influence of habitual karma from the past. Someone who says, "I can attain Buddhahood in this lifetime because my true nature is Buddha nature" *"fails to understand the influence of good and evil karma of past lives"* and *"that every evil act done - even as slight as a particle on the tip of a strand of rabbit's fur or sheep's wool - has its cause in past karma."*[91] In the same way as someone who abused drugs for many years thinks that he can give up immediately his dependency, and after a few tries he ends up taking a super dose, also *"a person may not wish to harm anyone and yet end up killing a hundred or a thousand people"*[92]. This is the heavy influence of karma from past lives and it is exactly why we need Amida's helping hand. The salvation promised in His Primal Vow does not depend on our own will which is weakened by our bad karma from past lives, but on Amida's Power of curing our illnesses and transforming us into Buddhas: *"it is by the inconceivable working of the Vow* (or *"the mysterious power of the Primal Vow"*, as Honen said) *that we are saved"*[93].

If you were born a woman, don't try to become a man, and if you were born a man, don't try to become a woman, as some deluded people do nowadays. Men and women are equally saved by Amida and they both will become splendid Buddhas in His Pure Land, going forever beyond manhood and womanhood. If you are a grave sinner don't think you are excluded, and if you believe you have some kind of wisdom or goodness within you, don't think that is the same with the

---

[91] Shinran Shonin, The *Collected Works of Shinran*, Shin Buddhism Translation Series, Jodo Shinshu Hongwanji-ha, Kyoto, 1997, p.670
[92] Shinran Shonin, The *Collected Works of Shinran*, Shin Buddhism Translation Series, Jodo Shinshu Hongwanji-ha, Kyoto, 1997, p.671
[93] Shinran Shonin, The *Collected Works of Shinran*, Shin Buddhism Translation Series, Jodo Shinshu Hongwanji-ha, Kyoto, 1997, p.671

supramundane wisdom and merits of Amida, but entrust to Him like any evil and stupid person because when compared with a Buddha we are all sinners and ignorant.

What does pious or irreligious mean in the above passage? The pious is, for example, the one who attends many services at home or in the temple, goes into pilgrimages, etc, while the irreligious is the one who does not have a strict religious schedule and discipline. Both are saved as long as they say the Nembutsu of faith.

Although the Power invested in the Primal Vow and in Amida's Name is impossible to understand with our limited unenlightened minds, we can easily grasp the meaning of Amida's requirements for us: "entrust to me, say my Name and wish to be born in my land". Both the wise and the idiots can understand these, especially if they are not obstructed by false teachers who complicate things. Also, Namo Amida Bu means "I take refuge in Amida Buddha/Homage to Amida Buddha" which is also extremely simple to understand and pronounce. One can even choose from among the various Nembutsu formulas like Namo Amitabha, Namo Amituofo, Namo Adidaphat, Namo Amida Bu (tsu), etc, or even say it in one's own language.

All learning and scholarship are equal to zero in matters related with birth in the Pure Land (Ojo) which is obtained with a simple faith in Amida. Honen expressed this so well at the end of his answer:

"All I have learned in my studies through the years is absolutely without avail in procuring me Ojo, and the one thing learning has taught me is its utter powerlessness to bring me Ojo",

His words made me remember Master Rennyo who also said that knowledge is useless for one who didn't solve the matter of his after life through faith in Amida:

"It has been said that those who do not know the importance of the afterlife are foolish, even though they may understand eighty thousand sutras and teachings; those who know about the afterlife[94] are wise, even though they may be unlettered men and women."[95]

---

[94] *"Those who know about the afterlife"* are those who know where they go after death – that is, in the Pure Land of Amida, due to entrusting to Him during their present life.

[95] Rennyo Shonin Ofumi: The Letters of Rennyo, translated from the Japanese (Taisho, Volume 74, Number 2668) by Ann T. Rogers and Minor L. Rogers, Numata Center for Buddhist Translation and Research, Berkeley, California, 1996, p.107

Soldiers are saved by Amida Buddha if they entrust to Him (Honen Shonin's instructions to Samurai Taro Tadatsuma Amakasu)

In the province of Musashi there lived a samurai called Taro Tadatsuna Amakasu, who belonged to the Inomata clan and was in the service of the Minamoto family. He was also a devout Nembutsu follower of Honen Shonin. At that time there was a conflict with the warrior monks armies of Mount Hiei who took their stand at the Hiyosho Hachioji shrine. Tadatsuna was put by Imperial command in charge of a body of troops to suppress the uprising. Before going to battle he paid a visit to Honen and said to him:

*"I have often heard you say that even sinners like us, if they will only say the Nembutsu, and put their whole trust in Amida's Primal Vow, will undoubtedly attain Ojo (birth in the Pure Land). This has made a deep impression upon me, but **I suppose it is the case only with those who are lying on a sick bed and calmly waiting for the end to come**. But as for myself, being a samurai, I cannot do just as I would like, and now in obedience to an imperial order, I am setting out for the castle at Hachioji to chastise those obstreperous priests of Sammon. I was born in a soldier's family and trained in the use of the bow and arrow, being on the one hand under obligation not to fail in carrying out at least in some measure the will of my ancestors, and on the other responsible for handling down something of glory to my posterity. **And yet if, as a soldier, I abandon myself to the driving back of the enemy, all sorts of wicked and**

*furious passions are likely to be stirred within me, and it becomes very hard to awaken any pious feeling in my heart. If, indeed, I should allow myself to keep **thinking all the time about the transitoriness of life**, and **trying not to forget the truth about attaining Ojo by the Nembutsu**, I should be in danger of being taken captive by my enemies, and thereby be eternally branded as a coward, straightway have all my patrimony confiscated, and so for a fool like me it is very hard to decide which of these courses to choose. Will you not tell me **how I may accomplish my cherished desire for Ojo, without on the other hand sacrificing the honor of my family as an archer?"***

To this Honen made the following reply:
*'Amida's Primal Vow says nothing about whether a man is good or bad, nor does it discuss whether a man's religious practices are many or few. It makes no discrimination between the pure and the impure, and takes no account of time, space or any other diverse circumstances of men's lives. **It matters not how a man dies**. The wicked man, just as he is, will attain Ojo if he calls on the sacred Name. This is the wonderful thing about Amida's Primal Vow. And so, though a man born in an archer's family goes to war, and loses his life, if he only repeats the sacred Name and relies upon Amida's Primal Vow, there is not the slightest doubt whatever that Amida will come to welcome him to His Pure Land'.*

Under these gentle instructions his doubts left him, and with a glad heart he exclaimed: 'Tadatsuma's birth into the Pure Land will verily take place today'.

Honen handed him a sacred scarf which he put under his armor, and he finally set out for the castle at Hachioji, where he abandoned himself to battle with the rioters. In the midst of the struggle his sword was broken, and he received a deep wound. Seeing it was quite hopeless, he flung down his sword, and clasping his hands, with a loud voice he called upon the sacred Name, and gave himself over to into the hands of the enemy. Purple clouds covered the battlefield and many smelled the delicious perfume, and people said that purple clouds also hung over the northern mountain. When Honen heard about it, 'Good' said he, 'Amakasu has been born into the Pure Land.'

His wife, who stayed at home in his native province, dreamt that he appeared to her in the act of attaining Ojo, and startled at the dream, she at once dispatched a messenger to the scene of battle, who on his way met a messenger coming to tell the news of Amakasu's death to his wife. They talked together, the one of the dream far away in the country, and the other of the way in which he had attained Ojo on the battlefield. Is it not indeed a remarkable coincidence?
On the one hand he attained Ojo as he gave his life on the field of battle, and on the other he maintained the glory of his ancestors. Both illustrate the profound meaning of the Primal Vow, and at the same time the force of Honen's teaching and example."[96]

---

[96] Honen the Buddhist Saint - His Life and Teachings, volume III, compiled by imperial order, translation by Rev Ryugaku Ishizuka and Rev Harper Havelock Coates, The Society for the Publication of Sacred Books of the World, Kyoto, 1949, p. 475-477

Commentary:
It is important to understand that Honen did not justify war nor did he discuss whether the war led by Amakasu was right or not, or if his enemies were evil or innocent. He didn't try to convince the samurai to be peaceful, didn't give him some moral speeches and he didn't tell him that so-called glory or honor are illusions and actually mean nothing from the point of view of ultimate reality. Why? Because it was useless. Would Amakasu gave up going to war if Honen had a different approach? No, so why insist on that when he knew that a soldier like him could not disobey orders and was so much entangled in his illusory self-created warrior personality? Only two things were in Honen's wise and compassionate mind:
1) war is part of samsara and thus, it is unavoidable and
2) how to save Amakasu, given his incapacity to destroy his illusions and blind passions.

The goal of Buddha Dharma is to bring everybody to perfect Enlightenment. Attention here – EVERYBODY! Not only the spiritual elite, the peaceful, the smiling saint or the good and detached people, but especially those who cannot overcome their blind passions and egotism.
How can a soldier whose mind is focused on the enemy, hating and killing, can attain perfect Enlightenment through his own power? Amakasu was himself aware of the evil inside and knew that he could not develop any pious feeling – *"all sorts of wicked and furious passions are likely to be stirred within me, and it becomes very hard to awaken any pious feeling in my heart"*.

In the chaos of battle nobody can contemplate Buddhist truths or stop fighting to develop some special feeling in relation with Amida and Nembutsu, or meditate on the meaning of the Pure Land teaching. Doing that would lead to lack of focus and a dishonorable capture which would have very bad consequences for Amakasu's family. Honen's answer assured him that there is no such requirement in the Primal Vow. Amida Buddha takes people from where they are, NOT from where they supposed to be. The goal of Buddhahood, perfect wisdom and perfect compassion is nice and desirable but here and now we are evil, we hate, we fight, and even kill others in war. Especially for such people who cannot abstain from evil and cannot save themselves, the Primal Vow was made.

Amida is not a Nordic god who praises war, and the Pure land is not Valhalla to be achieved by courage and dying in battle. One can lead the life of a warrior with all the worldly concepts of glory, honor, duty and ancestors' pride or he can be a coward and still be saved by Him. Amida regards all worldly affairs and activities of unenlightened beings as events in a dream, and does His best to pull them out of their never-ending suffering. His focus is on saving, not judging. Yes, killing is evil, but this is samsara, not the Pure Land. No Buddha agrees with killing and making sentient beings suffer, but as I said, Amida is focused on saving, not judging, and YES, Amida saves warriors, too. I do not wish to enter into any philosophical arguments whether war is necessary or not, or if it can be justified (we should remember that Hitler was not defeated with flowers…) but simply want to point out that Amida Buddha is saving everybody who entrusts to Him, say His Name and wish to go to His Pure Land. This is all that is required from us in His Primal Vow and Honen emphasized this to Amakasu:

"Amida's Primal Vow says nothing about whether a man is good or bad, nor does it discuss whether a man's religious practices are many or few[97]. It makes no discrimination between the pure and the impure, and takes no account of time, space or any other diverse circumstances of men's lives."

Amida wants to save us and is focused on saving us. I am never tired on repeating this, so that people understand it and realize they are accepted as they are. Being saved as we are does NOT mean Amida agrees with our evil minds and evil actions and it does NOT mean that evil is not evil or that wrong is right. It simply means Amida has Infinite compassion for us and loves us unconditionally. He made a Vow to create the karmic causes to take us out of samsara. A firefighter saves all people caught in a house on fire without checking if they are good or evil. He just goes there and saves them, which is exactly what Amida does with us. All that matters is that we accept His helping hand which is what the Nembutsu of faith is all about. Namo Amida Bu – I take refuge in Amida Buddha/I accept Amida's salvation.

---

[97] Amida is not impressed by one's spiritual practices and does not recquire us to to anything else than entrust to Him, say His Name in faith and wish to be born in His Pure Land.

If one says this Nembutsu he will attain Ojo (birth in the Pure Land) no matter how he dies – in one's own bed or in war, in the street or in the hospital, if he dies as a brave man or afraid and crying, if he has many virtues or none at all. *"It matters not how a man dies"* said Honen Shonin and his disciple Shinran was in agreement with him:

"I, for my own part, attach no significance to the condition, good or bad, of persons in their final moments. People in whom shinjin is determined do not doubt, and so abide among the truly settled. For this reason, their end also - even for those ignorant and foolish and lacking in wisdom - is a happy one."[98]

This is indeed, *"the wonderful thing about Amida's Primal Vow"*.

As a person of faith, the samurai Taro Tadatsuna Amakasu went to war and fought hard. Then with sword broken and mortally wounded he put his hands in gassho and said the Nembutsu, thus entering the Pure Land of Amida. He did not dishonor his ancestors and he became a splendid Buddha.

While the Primal Vow is beyond any samsaric and illusory concepts of honor and glory, it doesn't prevent one from achieving them. One can love his country, fight and die for it and be remembered for many generations while also be saved by Amida and enter His Pure Land.

---

[98] The Collected Works of Shinran, Shin Buddhism Translation Series, Jodo Shinshu Hongwanji-ha, Kyoto, 1997, p.531

If possible, try to avoid war and killing, but if you must go to war then keep this teaching into your heart and say the Nembutsu of faith. If you die in battle, you will attain Ojo and then you will be able to work as a Buddha, for the salvation of those you killed.
Namo Amida Bu

The prostitute of Muro

"When Honen arrived at the port of Muro on his way into exile on Shikoku in the spring of 1207, a small boat drew near carrying a woman of the night. She said to Honen, 'I heard that this was your boat, and I have come to meet you. There are many ways of getting on in the world, but what terrible acts could have been committed in a former life of mine to bring me into such a miserable life as this? What can a woman who carries a load of karma like mine do to escape and be saved in the world to come?'

Honen compassionately replied, 'Your guilt in living such a life is surely great and the [karmic] penalties seem incalculable. If you can find another means of livelihood, give this up at once. But if you can't, or if you are not yet ready to sacrifice your very life for the true way, begin just as you are and call on the sacred Name (Namo Amida Bu). It is for just such deluded folk as you that Amida Buddha made that wonderfully comprehensive Primal Vow. So put your full trust in it without the smallest reservation. If you rely upon the Primal Vow and repeat the Nembutsu, your Ojo (birth in the Pure Land) is absolutely certain.' Thus kindly taught, the woman began to weep out of joy. Later, Honen said of her, 'She is a woman of strong faith. She is sure to attain Ojo.'

A year later when he was returning to the capital after his exile, Honen called at this place again and inquired about her. He found out that from the time he had instructed her, she had retired to a village near the mountains and had been devoting herself to the practice of the Nembutsu. A short time after, as death drew near, it was with great composure that she safely accomplished her Ojo (birth in the Pure Land). On being told this, Honen said, 'Yes, it is just as I had expected.'"[99]

Commentary:
As we have seen, first Honen encourages her to change her ways. He does not tell her that being a prostitute is good, but on the contrary: *"Your guilt in living such a life is surely great and the [karmic] penalties seem incalculable. If you can find another means of livelihood, give this up at once"*. Amida Dharma is not an encouragement to do evil or lead an immoral life (she actually practices one form of sexual misconduct), so everyone should try his/her best to change.

However, his intention is not to judge her, nor make her despair, but to lead her to salvation, so he immediately points to the Primal Vow of Amida Buddha who discriminates against nobody and is especially addressed to the lowest of the low: *"But if you can't, or if you are not yet ready to sacrifice your very life for the true way, begin just as you are and call on the sacred Name. It is for just such deluded folk as you that Amida Buddha made that wonderfully comprehensive Primal Vow"*.

---

[99] Source of the passage, http://jsri.jp/English/Main.html

This is the beauty of our Path - we are not spoiled by, nor told that we are great or that our ways are good when they aren't, but showed the consequences of our choices and offered the only escape available for people like us - Amida's Primal Vow: "entrust yourself to me, say my Name and wish to be born in my land".

Namo Amida Bu

The indiscriminative salvation offered by Amida Buddha is not an encouragement to commit or justify evil

"There are those who say that the effort to avoid sin and improve oneself is making light of Amida's Vow [...] But do not for a moment be misled by such misconceptions. Is there any place in any of the sutras where Amida encourages men to sin? Certainly not. Such things come from those who make no effort to get away from their own evil deeds, and who go on in their former sinful life. By such utterly unreasonable and false sayings, they would mislead ignorant men and women, urging them forward in the committing of sin and stirring up their evil passions within them. Now such persons are nothing less than a company of devil, and you ought to think of them as enemies to your reaching birth into the Pure Land of Bliss".[100]

Commentary:
It is extremely important to understand that Amida Dharma is not an instrument to justify blind passions nor institutionalize them as normal behavior. Indeed, in its saving activity, Amida Buddha makes no distinction between virtuous and non-virtuous people. But making no distinction, out of Great Compassion, between them, does not mean that He supports or encourages evil. No Buddha, including Amida and Shakyamuni, have ever

---

[100] Honen the Buddhist Saint - His Life and Teachings, volume III, compiled by imperial order, translation by Rev Ryugaku Ishizuka and Rev Harper Havelock Coates, The Society for the Publication of Sacred Books of the World, Kyoto, 1949, p. 404-405

supported evil actions. Please do not confuse being saved as you are with the idea that all your actions are now worthy and good or that you should not make any effort for good behavior. Instead of praising or justifying your blind passions, be ashamed of them and grateful to Amida's helping hand. As Shinran said, *"don't take a liking to poison because you have the antidote"*, that is, try your best to abandon evil actions even if you are saved by Amida.

Sinners are saved if they accept themselves to be sinners in need of salvation. But one cannot be saved if he constantly tries to find justification for his evil deeds or if he uses the Amida Dharma and the Buddhist temples to promote or institutionalize immoral behavior.

The Buddhist precepts are a mirror through which we can realize how wretched we are and how much we need to entrust to Amida Buddha. Reading about precepts is like a good slap in the face to our arrogant ego that often wanders here and there doing, saying and thinking all kinds of immoral things. Of course, the Buddhist morality is not something to be easily liked by our samsaric minds as we often tend to find excuses and make efforts to forget when we do a bad thing or to pretend that we actually had good intentions. However, the Mahayana precepts help us come face to face with who we really are. I always bow in humility and shame when reading about the high moral ideal of Mahayana. Precepts remind me of how much I need Amida and how truly compassionate is His Primal Vow.

The truth is that we don't need to change Buddhist morality when we are saved as we are by Amida Buddha. I'm sure nobody likes to be told he is a sinner but this is exactly what we need to be reminded very often. Somebody must tell us that we are not as good as we think we are, that goodness is not an ideological construct of this or that sexual, social or political ideology and that Buddhist morality does not change with times and fashion. We need Buddhist precepts to shake us out of our complacency and tell us what we do not want to hear so that we become aware of our evil within and accept Amida's helping hand.

Those who disregard Buddhist morality or want to change it according to their personal views are encouraging people to sin without the awareness of sin. To sin without being aware of sin is to do evil and immoral deeds while lying oneself and others that evil is good or that immorality is moral and normal. When one is presenting evil and immorality as being good and moral, he is actually urging others to commit evil and makes them incapable to look up to the salvation offered by Amida, making them think that they are good people without any need for salvation, or influences them to believe in heretical views such as Amida encouraging evil and immorality. In our present time many are already using Amida's Primal Vow to justify all kinds of unnatural behavior and transform temples into platforms for various deviant ideologies.

"Such persons are", according to Honen, *"nothing less than a company of devil, and you ought to think of them*

as enemies to your reaching birth into the Pure Land of Bliss."

Nembutsu and daily life

"If we only put our trust in Amida's Primal Vow, there is no doubt whatever about our future destiny, but what are we to do with the present world?'
'Well, the thing to do is to make the Nembutsu practice the chief thing in life, and to lay aside everything that you think may interfere with it. If you cannot stay in one spot and do it, then do it when you are walking. If you cannot do it as a priest, then do it as a layman. If you cannot do it alone, then do it in the company of others. If you cannot do it and at the same time provide yourself with food and clothing, then accept the help of others and go on doing it. Or if you cannot get others to help you, then look after yourself but keep on doing it. Your wife and children and domestics are for this very purpose, of helping you to practice it, and if they prove an obstacle, you ought not to have any. Friends and property are good, if they too prove helpful, but if they prove a hindrance they should be given up. In short, there is nothing that may not help us to Ojo, so long as it helps us to go on the even tenor of our way through life undisturbed.'"[101]

Commentary:
The goal of Buddhism is not to attain happiness here and now which is actually impossible as samsara itself is the karmic effect of our own blind passions and ignorance.

---

[101] Honen the Buddhist Saint - His Life and Teachings, volume V, compiled by imperial order, translation by Rev Ryugaku Ishizuka and Rev Harper Havelock Coates, The Society for the Publication of Sacred Books of the World, Kyoto, 1949, p. 737

However, this doesn't mean that we should neglect our basic needs. Amida devotees also eat, drink, seek shelter, comfort and good company, they get married, have children, property, etc. There is no problem with this. What Honen Shonin advised us is to use all the aspects of our life as support for the Nembutsu Path. The Primal Vow of Amida does not require asceticism, but only the Nembutsu of faith, so try to arrange your personal life in such a way that you are able to walk the Path of Nembutsu.

Honen's advice refers not only to the saying of Nembutsu, but also to all the aspects included in the religious life of a Nembutsu follower, like listening and studying the Dharma texts related to the Primal Vow and teaching or helping others to say this Nembutsu of faith. It's good to create the proper conditions in our life so that we can do all these without any internal or external obstruction. All obstructions are both external and internal as everything that interferes with the needs of our bodies will automatically affect our inner state of mind. If one is thirsty and hungry or cannot live without sex and the person he loves, he will be disturbed in mind and might not be able to focus on listening to Amida Dharma or teach others the way to salvation. If that is the case, then eat, drink, have sex and get married. This is why Shinran himself got married. On the contrary, if one feels that married life and children are an obstacle for his Nembutsu practice then he should not marry, not have children and live in seclusion.

Recently I advised a lady Nembutsu follower to divorce her husband because he forbade her to say Nembutsu and forced her to attend Christian church services and sacraments. I think that we should not make any concession to others in matters related to our birth in the Pure Land. We should never give up saying the Nembutsu because our family, friends or co-workers do not agree with it. We should never allow anybody to put obstacles of any kind on our Path to the Pure Land. If anybody becomes an obstruction to our religious life, we better walk away knowing that we can truly help and save them after we attain Buddhahood in the Pure Land.

Instead of being obsessed with purity and judge ourselves too harsh, we should be practical and acknowledge that we are ordinary beings with needs and attachments. Thus, we should know our limitations and have a strategy for a religious life that does not require superhuman efforts, especially that we follow a Path made for people of lower spiritual capacities. For example, I know somebody who constantly makes plans for long Nembutsu retreats but he can't live without modern comforts and his wife. What focus on liturgies and Dharma teaching can that person have in a retreat if he constantly mises her! So, I advised him to stop dreaming about retreats and instead come to the temple from time to time and say Nembutsu at home while enjoying his lovely wife and comfort. I mention that she has nothing against him being a Buddhist, so he can say Nembutsu as much as he wants at his personal altar.

Again, be honest about yourself and your limitations and arrange your life so as to be able to say the Nembutsu of faith, study the Amida Dharma and possibly help others entrust to Amida.

Treat the Nembutsu Path as the center of your life and anything else as means to help you focus on it.

Honen said the Nembutsu as if already saved by Amida

"Where one is to receive something from another, which is better, to have already received, or not yet to have received? I, Genku (Honen), repeat the Nembutsu as if I had already received."[102]

Commentary:
There are two types of Nembutsu: the Nembutsu of those who don't have faith, and the Nembutsu of faith.
The Nembutsu of those who are not yet established in faith is said without being sure of their salvation (*"not yet to have received"* – not yet assured of birth in the Pure Land). This is because when one relies on one's own power one cannot have any certainty.
The Nembutsu of faith or Honen's Nembutsu is said by one who knows that he has already received the assurance of birth in the Pure Land since the moment he entrusted for the first time in Amida *("have already received")*. This is the Nembutsu of Buddha centered Power through which one is certain to attain Ojo[103]. It is also the Nembutsu of "thank you Amida Buddha for saving me as I am".

---

[102] Honen the Buddhist Saint - His Life and Teachings, volume III, compiled by imperial order, translation by Rev Ryugaku Ishizuka and Rev Harper Havelock Coates, The Society for the Publication of Sacred Books of the World, Kyoto, 1949, p. 400
[103] Ojo means birth in the Pure Land.

Faith, Nembutsu and aspiration are one

"If one desires to attain birth in the Pure Land, both his heart and practice must be in concert. Therefore, the interpretation of Master Shan-tao reads: 'Practice alone is not sufficient for the accomplishment of birth in the Pure Land. Neither is aspiration alone. Realization occurs only when aspiration and practice are concomitant.'

Both heart and practice must be a single discipline, not only to achieve birth in the Pure Land, but also to realize Enlightenment in the Holy Gate. This is referred to as 'observing the practice by awakening the heart to Enlightenment'.

In Jodo Shu (Pure Land school), Master Shan-tao called this 'the steadfast heart and practice'."[104]

Commentary:
"Heart" refers to the "entrusting heart" (shinjin) or faith in Amida Buddha. This is also linked with *"aspiration"*, which is aspiration or desire to be born in the Pure Land. *"Practice"* is to say the Name of Amida Buddha.
All these three: faith (shinjin), the saying of the Name and the wish (*aspiration*) to be born in the Pure Land are the three requirements of Amida in His Primal Vow, where He asked beings to entrust to Him, say His Name and wish to be born in His Pure Land: *"sincerely entrust*

---

[104] Teachings of Honen, translated by Yoko Hayashi and Joji Atone, Los Angeles: Bukkyo University – Los Angeles Extension, 2007, p. 74.

themselves to me (faith/shinjin), desire to be born in my land (aspiration), and say my Name (Nembutsu) perhaps even ten times".

So, if these three combines, that is, if we say the Nembutsu as an expression of faith in Amida and we aspire to be born in His Pure Land, then we'll go there *("realization")*. If one of these is lacking, for example, if we say the Nembutsu without faith and without the wish (aspiration) to be born in the Pure Land, then we'll not go there. Same will happen if we wish to go to the Pure Land, pretend to have faith but do not say Nembutsu. I use the expression "pretend to have faith" because actually it's impossible to have faith and to aspire for the Pure Land but do not say the Nembutsu. You can't have faith and aspiration without Nembutsu, nor true Nembutsu[105] without faith and aspiration (wish) for the Pure Land. This is why Honen Shonin said:

"If one deeply believes (shinjin) in this vow of Amida Buddha and does not entertain any doubts about birth in the Pure Land through Nembutsu, ten out of ten and one hundred out of one hundred people will achieve birth in the Pure Land through just a single utterance of Nembutsu. Conversely, one who doubts birth in the Pure Land through Nembutsu will not attain this birth, even if this individual recites Nembutsu."[106]

---

[105] By true Nembutsu I mean the Nembutsu of the Primal Vow, the Nembtsu of total reliance on Amida Buddha's Power.

[106] Honen Shonin, *Essentials for Birth in the Pure Land through Nembutsu, The Promise of Amida Buddha - Honen's Path to Bliss*; English translation of the Genko edition of the works of Honen

His disciple, Shinran Shonin, who later continued his work, also explained:

"Though a person may have shinjin (faith), if he or she does not say the Name it is of no avail. And conversely, even though a person fervently says the Name, if that person's shinjin is shallow he cannot attain birth in the Pure Land. Thus, it is the person who both deeply entrusts himself to Birth through the Nembutsu and undertakes to say the Name who is certain to be born in the true fulfilled land[107]."[108]

*"Although the one moment of shinjin (faith) and the one moment of Nembutsu are two**, there is no Nembutsu separate from shinjin, nor is the one moment of shinjin separate from the one moment of Nembutsu.** The reason is that the practice of Nembutsu is to say it perhaps once, perhaps ten times, on hearing and*

Shonin - *Collected Teachings of Kurodani Shonin: The Japanese Anthology (Wago Toroku)*, translated by Joji Atone and Yoko Hayashi, Wisdom Publications, Boston, 2011, p.361

[107] This is the center of the Pure Land where he automatically attains perfect Enlightenment. It is attained through complete faith in the Power of Amida Buddha and is contrasted with birth in the border land where those who say Nembutsu while still clinging to their self-power may go if they are very serious in Nembutsu recitation up to the moment of their death. See my explanations of the border land in my books, especially in the *Commentary on the Sutra on the Buddha of Infinite Life* and *Jodo Shinshu Buddhist Teachings, 2nd revised edition.*

[108] Shinran Shonin, Lamp for the Latter-Ages, letter 12, *The Collected Works of Shinran*, Shin Buddhism Translation Series, Jodo Shinshu Hongwanji-ha, Kyoto, 1997, p.539

realizing that birth into the Pure Land is attained by saying the Name fulfilled in the Primal Vow. To hear this Vow and be completely without doubt is the one moment of shinjin. **Thus, although shinjin and Nembutsu are two, since shinjin (faith) is to hear and not doubt that you are saved by only a single pronouncing, which is the fulfillment of practice, there is no shinjin separate from Nembutsu**; *this is the teaching I have received (from Master Honen). You should know further that* **there can be no Nembutsu separate from shinjin. Both should be understood to be Amida's Vow.**"[109]

Others also agreed with Honen, Shan-tao and Shinran, like for example, Master Yuan-chao:

"*So long as you are resolute and unwavering in your faith, you will attain birth with ten utterances of the Nembutsu, even if sinister signs may appear at the end your life.*"[110]

And Master Chih-yüan of Mount Ku:

---

[109] Shinran Shonin, Lamp for the Latter-Ages, letter 11, *The Collected Works of Shinran*, Shin Buddhism Translation Series, Jodo Shinshu Hongwanji-ha, Kyoto, 1997, p.538

[110] Shinran Shonin quoted Master Yuan-chao in Kyogyoshinsho, III. *Kyogyoshinsho – On Teaching, Practice, Faith, and Enlightenment*, translated by Hisao Inagaki, Numata Center for Buddhist Translation and Research, Kyoto, 2003, p. 117

"Through the power of faith, one firmly accepts the Name in one's heart".[111]

Disciples of the self-power paths also need the unity between mind/heart/aspiration and practice. Honen mentioned that in their case, the unity is called *"observing the practice by awakening the heart to Enlightenment"* and specified that *"in Jodo Shu (Pure Land school), Master Shan-tao called this 'the steadfast heart and practice'"*. In the online Cambridge dictionary, we read that steadfast means *"staying the same for a long time and not changing quickly or unexpectedly"*. Indeed, the heart/mind of one who entrusts to Amida Buddha NEVER changes during our lifetime and our saying of the Name in faith, although not dependent on a fix number, continues until death.

On the Pure Land Path, we are also taught that faith (shinjin) is itself the Bodhi Mind or the mind to aspire for Enlightenment as we know that after we reach the Pure Land through the Nembutsu of faith we attain perfect Enlightenment (Buddhahood/Nirvana). In this regard, Shinran Shonin said:

"The mind that aspires to attain Buddhahood
Is the mind to save all sentient beings;
The mind to save all sentient beings
Is true and real shinjin (faith), which is Amida's benefiting of others.

---

[111] Shinran quoted Master Chih-yüan of Mount Ku in his Kyogyoshinsho, VI. *Kyogyoshinsho – On Teaching, Practice, Faith, and Enlightenment*, translated by Hisao Inagaki, Numata Center for Buddhist Translation and Research, Kyoto, 2003, p. 117

Shinjin is the mind that is single;
The mind that is single is the diamondlike mind.
The diamondlike mind is the mind aspiring for
enlightenment (Bodhi Mind);
This mind is itself Other Power."[112]

---

[112] *The Collected Works of Shinran*, Shin Buddhism Translation Series, Jodo Shinshu Hongwanji-ha, Kyoto, 1997, p.365

Say the Nembutsu with an undivided mind

"I beg of you to believe with ever-deepening fervour, and with undivided mind to give yourself up to the Nembutsu."[113]
Honen Shonin

Commentary:
Here we can see again that Honen linked the saying of the Name with faith (shinjin), so the Nembutsu he always urged us to say was the Nembutsu of faith - the Nembutsu centered on Amida's Power. That Nembutsu is said with an undivided mind which means it is not mixed with other practices and faiths. The salvation offered by Amida Buddha takes place according to the law of karma, so in order to be saved we need to enter into karmic connection with Him. That can be done only if we have exclusive faith in Amida and say only His Name. This is the „undivided mind" Honen speaks about. Focus exclusively on Amida and abandon any reliance on other religious characters from inside or outside Buddhism. All Buddhas are automatically praised when you say the Name of Amida, and non-Buddhist divinities are deluded samsaric beings, so they cannot be an object of refuge.

---

[113] Honen the Buddhist Saint - His Life and Teachings, volume III, compiled by imperial order, translation by Rev Ryugaku Ishizuka and Rev Harper Havelock Coates, The Society for the Publication of Sacred Books of the World, Kyoto, 1949, p. 468

The number of Nembutsu recitation is not important as long as we rely on Amida's Power

There are some who teach that Nembutsu must be said many times in order to reach birth in the Pure Land, thus forgetting the Power behind the Name which makes the Nembutsu effective. I would ask these people to try using their own names, John, Marc, Mary, etc, and see if they can attain birth in the Pure Land through them. Of course they can't, and the reason why is that theirs are empty names without any power.

As the Nembutsu is the saying of Amida's Name it belongs to Amida and is infused with His infinite merits and Power. This is why it works in bringing us to the Pure Land at the end of our physical bodies. So, it is extremely important that our saying of the Name should be an expression of faith in Amida, and NOT in our capacities to say it often or seldom.

Each of us has his/her own personal relation with Amida Buddha who saves us one by one, having us always in front of His compassionate eyes. We do not need to be heroes, have the same visions or recitation capacities like Masters of the past, but simply say the Nembutsu according to our personal conditions while keeping in mind that Amida did NOT impose a fixed number of recitations in order to be born in His Pure Land: *"say my Name perhaps even ten times"*. This expression *"perhaps even ten times"* means ANY NUMBER from one to ten or to hundreds, thousands and as many as we can.

Honen Shonin explained:

"Master Shan-tao earnestly practiced the vocal Nembutsu without stopping until he was completely spent. He repeated Nembutsu to the extent that he perspired in the freezing cold. [...] We may think that only those who have a dauntless and bold heart, such as Master Shan-tao, whose authenticity is supreme, could achieve birth in the Pure Land and that the rest of us could not. [...] The rest of all sentient beings, like us, need not compare ourselves with him in order to achieve birth in the Pure Land."[114]

So, be yourself in your relation with Amida Buddha, relax and say His Name according to your situation. As Amida himself does not compare you with others, why would you do it?

Here is a very important passage from Honen's *Essential Discourse on Birth in the Pure Land through Nembutsu*:

" Question: Which is superior in merit: a mere single utterance of Nembutsu or ten repetitions of Nembutsu?

---

[114] Honen Shonin, An Outline of the Doctrine for Birth in the Pure Land. *The Promise of Amida Buddha - Honen's Path to Bliss*; English translation of the Genko edition of the works of Honen Shonin - *Collected Teachings of Kurodani Shonin: The Japanese Anthology (Wago Toroku)*, translated by Joji Atone and Yoko Hayashi, Wisdom Publications, Boston, 2011, p.101

Answer: They have the same merit with regard to birth in the Pure Land"[115].
Why do they have the same merit? Because the merit is in Amida himself and only Amida owns the merits of His own Name. This is also why ten thousand repetitions are the same as one or ten – because, I repeat, **the merit belongs to Amida!** Thus, Honen said:

"The number of recitations is not the issue".[116]

His disciple Shinran, also said:

"In the Primal Vow are the words:
'Saying my Name perhaps even ten times'.

Know from the words 'ten times' that appear from the beginning in the Vow itself that saying the Name is not limited to one utterance. And the word 'perhaps even'

---

[115] Honen Shonin, Essential Discourse on Birth in the Pure Land through Nembutsu. *The Promise of Amida Buddha - Honen's Path to Bliss*; English translation of the Genko edition of the works of Honen Shonin - *Collected Teachings of Kurodani Shonin: The Japanese Anthology (Wago Toroku)*, translated by Joji Atone and Yoko Hayashi, Wisdom Publications, Boston, 2011, p.124

[116] Honen Shonin, Essential Discourse on Birth in the Pure Land through Nembutsu. *The Promise of Amida Buddha - Honen's Path to Bliss*; English translation of the Genko edition of the works of Honen Shonin - *Collected Teachings of Kurodani Shonin: The Japanese Anthology (Wago Toroku)*, translated by Joji Atone and Yoko Hayashi, Wisdom Publications, Boston, 2011, p.124-125

makes it clearer still that there is no set number of times one should say the Name."[117]

It saddens me to see how people often forget that in the Primal Vow, Amida mentioned the saying of His Name **in relation with faith**: *"sincerely **entrust themselves to me**, desire to be born in my land, and say my Name perhaps even ten times"*. Thus, it is ONLY if one has faith in Amida that the saying of His Name is effective in fulfilling one's desire to be born in the Pure Land. Unfortunately, many nowadays have faith in themselves when they say Amida's Name, so they think that their mental or verbal capacities are essential for birth in the Pure Land. This is similar with changing the wording of the Primal Vow into something like: "sincerely entrust to yourself and say my Name perhaps even ten times".

You might be surprised to find that not only those who think the Name must be said many times are attached to their self-power but even those who think the Name must be said once or a few times only. Any "must" in relation with the number of Nembutsu is a heresy from the point of view of Honen, Shinran and the Primal Vow itself. Both those who advocate the doctrine of many-callings of the Name or the doctrine of once-calling are attached to their own power, thinking that somehow Amida's work of salvation can be improved or obstructed by saying His Name many times. Both

---

[117] Shinran Shonin, Notes on Once-Calling and Many-Calling, The Collected Works of Shinran, Shin Buddhism Translation Series, Jodo Shinshu Hongwanji-ha, Kyoto, 1997, p.482

categories are focused on themselves and not on Amida who is the only real Power behind His Name.

Honen said:

"There seem to be many who say that reciting Nembutsu sixty thousand times a day and repeating Nembutsu as many times as possible will be to doubt the compassionate power of Amida Buddha. Don't lend an ear to such misguided notions. [...]

It is a grave misconception to call someone who recites Nembutsu many times as a 'practitioner of nembutsu with self-power.' Someone who recites Nembutsu merely once or twice, relying on his own efforts, is referred to as a devotee of nembutsu with self-power. Conversely, if one recites Nembutsu continually one thousand or ten thousand times each day and night for one hundred or one thousand days, **with complete reliance on the power of the Primal Vow** *and with respect for the compassionate power of Amida Buddha, this Nembutsu, with each mindful utterance, is considered to be Nembutsu with Other Power."*[118]

The only aspect that makes the difference between false nembutsu and true Nembutsu is not to be found in the

---

[118] Honen Shonin, Instruction in the Seven Articles. *The Promise of Amida Buddha - Honen's Path to Bliss*; English translation of the Genko edition of the works of Honen Shonin - *Collected Teachings of Kurodani Shonin: The Japanese Anthology (Wago Toroku)*, translated by Joji Atone and Yoko Hayashi, Wisdom Publications, Boston, 2011, p.137

number but in having or not having faith - *"complete reliance on the power of the Primal Vow"*. *"Mindful utterance"* means that one is mindful of Amida's Power which means he knows that his Nembutsu recitation is effective because of Amida, not his personal capacities.

I myself have days when I say Nembutsu many times and when I say it a few times, but in both situations, I do not forget that it is Amida Buddha himself who makes my one or ten or a thousand recitations effective in bringing me to the Pure Land, not the movement of my lips, my focus, or any so-called spiritual capacities and fake goodness that can be found within myself.

Please also read my detailed explanations on this topic of once-calling and many-callings of Amida's Name in my book *The Meaning of Faith and Nembutsu in Jodo Shinshu Buddhism*.

Remember to say the Nembutsu

"You must believe that Nembutsu possesses supreme merit and that Amida Buddha with His great compassion of the Primal Vow, will come to embrace one who recites Nembutsu even ten times or just once. Thus, believing this, practice Nembutsu for your entire lifetime without negligence"[119].

Commentary:
As I showed in chapter "The Nembutsu is true and real" from my book *Simple Teachings on Emptiness and Buddha nature*, by quoting many sacred texts, the Name contains the merits of Amida and all Buddhas, as well as the virtues of all Buddhist teachings and practices. *"It is the treasure-sea of merits of true Suchness, ultimate reality"*[120], as Shinran said.

Also, Amida protects and embraces those who entrust to Him both in this life as well as in the moment of death when He welcomes them into His Pure Land of Bliss.

After pointing out that the number of recitations is not important for our birth in the Pure Land, Master Honen encouraged us to say the Name for our entire lifetime.

---

[119] *Teachings of Honen*, translated by Yoko Hayashi and Joji Atone, Bukkyo University, Los Angeles, p 243-245

[120] Shinran Shonin, Kyogyoshinsho, chapter II, Kyogyoshinsho – On Teaching, Practice, Faith, and Enlightenment, translated by Hisao Inagaki, Numata Center for Buddhist Translation and Research, Kyoto, 2003, p. 9

Just as one who was saved from fire will always be grateful to his savior, we should also not be negligent in expressing our gratitude to Amida Buddha for saving us from the repeated births and deaths. This is the reason why sometimes Honen, but also Shinran and Rennyo, insisted on remembering to say the Nembutsu. It was NOT that the number of recitations is important (it isn't!), but because we should remember to say "thank you" to the one who assured our liberation from samsara. The Nembutsu is also the expression of faith, so if we really entrusted ourselves to Amida, we'll surely like to express it by saying His Name.

The cause for birth into the Pure Land may appear anytime

Honen Shonin said:

"The completion of the karma necessary for birth into the Pure Land may be at any ordinary time, or at the time of death. There is no distinction made between the two in the language of the Primal Vow."[121]

In the very first moment one entrusts to Amida Buddha he enters the stage of no-retrogression for birth in the Pure Land where he will attain supreme Enlightenment. The karma necessary for birth into the Pure Land appears in the very first moment of faith when the believer receives the pure karmic merits of Amida which make him capable of going there.

This passage contradicts those who think that the moment of death is of paramount importance for birth into the Pure Land. I always insist that we are the school of the Primal Vow and that whatever we need to know is to be found in the Primal Vow. Honen Shonin thought the same when he made reference to *"the language of the Primal Vow"* in which Amida urged us to entrust to Him, say His Name and wish to be born in His land. Some do this when they are strong and healthy, young or old, while others when they are about to die. Amida did

---

[121] Honen the Buddhist Saint - His Life and Teachings, volume III, compiled by imperial order, translation by Rev Ryugaku Ishizuka and Rev Harper Havelock Coates, The Society for the Publication of Sacred Books of the World, Kyoto, 1949, p. 398

not mention a specific moment in life when one should entrust to Him, say His Name and wish to be born in His land, so we should not worry about this. Anytime is a good time to say the Nembutsu of faith.

The following passage proves even more that Honen Shonin did not add a special significance to the Nembutsu at the time of death:

"Question: Which is more profound: Nembutsu at the time of death or Nembutsu in our daily life?
Answer: They are the same. Our daily Nembutsu and Nembutsu at the time of death are no different at all. When we are visited by death, our daily Nembutsu becomes Nembutsu at death; if our life is prolonged, Nembutsu at death becomes Nembutsu of daily life."[122]

---

[122] *The Promise of Amida Buddha - Honen's Path to Bliss*; English translation of the Genko edition of the works of Honen Shonin - *Collected Teachings of Kurodani Shonin: The Japanese Anthology (Wago Toroku)*, translated by Joji Atone and Yoko Hayashi, Wisdom Publications, Boston, 2011, p.125

Do not mix Nembutsu with other practices

"The profound heart is the heart that believes profoundly in Nembutsu. It also means to recite exclusively Nembutsu without embracing other practices. If other practices are performed concurrently with Nembutsu, one would be a Nembutsu devotee lacking in the profound heart. To understand that the Three Sutras of Pure Land Buddhism taught by Buddha Shakyamuni exclusively propagate the sole practice of Nembutsu, to believe that the essence of the forty-eight vows of Amida Buddha is the Vow of the exclusive recitation of Nembutsu, and to recite single-heartedly Nembutsu - these indicate having the profound heart."[123]

Commentary:
We are the school of the Primal Vow. All we need to know and all we have to do for our salvation is found in the Primal Vow. This is why I explained it word by word in almost 90 pages in my *Commentary on Sutra on the Buddha of Infinite Life*.

We cannot enter into karmic connection with Amida Buddha for birth in the fulfilled land of the Pure Land[124]

---

[123] Honen Shonin, Instruction in the Seven Articles, *The Promise of Amida Buddha - Honen's Path to Bliss*; English translation of the Genko edition of the works of Honen Shonin - *Collected Teachings of Kurodani Shonin: The Japanese Anthology (Wago Toroku)*, translated by Joji Atone and Yoko Hayashi, Wisdom Publications, Boston, 2011, p.135

[124] This is the center of the Pure Land where perfect Enlightenment is attained instantly. The cause of birth there is complete faith in the

if we do not do EXACTLY what He asked us to do in His Primal Vow – entrust to Him, say His Name and wish to be born in His Pure Land. These three elements are exclusive requirements so we must have faith only in Amida, say only His Name and wish to be born only in His Pure Land. If we do exactly this and only this, then we receive the karma for birth there after death.

We must understand that everything is cause and effect, including birth in the Pure Land, so we cannot go there if we do not have the karma for this. The Path to Sukhavati[125] is extremely easy because it has the karmic cause in Amida Buddha himself, the Master of that Land. Thus, only if we are focused exclusively on Him, we can receive the karmic energy (merit) to go there.
It is like connecting your computer to a power source. The computer will automatically receive energy and will start working. The same happens to those who exclusively say Amida's Name in faith – they are connected to the only Power-source of the Pure Land, and they automatically receive the karmic energy to go there after death. We call this karmic energy – the merit transference from Amida to the devotee. Just like a car needs gas, a mind-stream needs to receive the merit

---

Power of Amida Buddha and is contrasted with birth in the border land where those who say Nembutsu while still clinging to their self-power may go if they are very serious in Nembutsu recitation up to the moment of their death. See my explanations of the border land in my books, especially in the *Commentary on the Sutra on the Buddha of Infinite Life* and *Jodo Shinshu Buddhist Teachings, 2nd revised edition.*

[125] Sukhavati is the Sanskrit name for the Pure Land and it means the Land of Bliss.

transference from Amida to enter the stage of non-retrogression for birth in the Pure Land.

Master Shan-tao said:

"Abandon the teachings that Amida Buddha abandoned, observe the practice that Amida Buddha observed, and leave the practices that Amida Buddha left. This is said to be 'in accordance with the teaching of Amida Buddha' and 'in compliance with the intent of Amida Buddha'. Such a person is referred to as the 'true disciple of Amida Buddha'".[126]

This passage is in agreement with Honen's above saying and it means that we must abandon everything which is not mentioned in the Primal Vow, where only faith, saying of the Name in faith and wish for birth in the Pure Land are taught. If you do this, you are in accord with Amida Buddha's Primal Vow and you are a true disciple of Amida Buddha. Any practice or teaching which are not mentioned in the Primal Vow, like various meditation methods, mantras or anything else, should not be followed because they do not lead to birth in the fulfilled land of the Pure Land.

To feel that the Name of Amida Buddha is somehow not enough for your religious life, is a sign that faith

---

[126] *The Promise of Amida Buddha - Honen's Path to Bliss*; English translation of the Genko edition of the works of Honen Shonin - *Collected Teachings of Kurodani Shonin: The Japanese Anthology (Wago Toroku)*, translated by Joji Atone and Yoko Hayashi, Wisdom Publications, Boston, 2011, p.106

(shinjin) is not yet firmly established in your heart. A true Amida devotee never feels something is lacking and is completely satisfied to say Amida's Name alone. He will never feel the need to add this or that meditation practice or this or that sacred mantra to his daily Nembutsu, and he will not pray to various gods and spirits. In the Primal Vow Amida Buddha presented the guidelines for our religious life, "entrust yourself to me, say my Name, and wish to be born in my land". So, we should do nothing else, but entrust to Amida Buddha, say His Name in faith and wish to be born in His Land after death.

Honen Shonin explained:

"'Leave what Amida Buddha left' is to leave aside the teachings, understandings, miscellaneous karmic conditions, and aberrant thought diverging from the Nembutsu tradition. Master Shan-tao reprimanded, 'They become hindrances not only to one's own attainment of birth in the Pure Land but to others' right practice for birth in the Pure Land'. These hindrances are frightening"[127].

---

[127] Honen Shonin, An Outline of the Doctrine for Birth in the Pure Land.*The Promise of Amida Buddha - Honen's Path to Bliss*; English translation of the Genko edition of the works of Honen Shonin - *Collected Teachings of Kurodani Shonin: The Japanese Anthology (Wago Toroku)*, translated by Joji Atone and Yoko Hayashi, Wisdom Publications, Boston, 2011, p.112

Especially if one is a teacher of Amida Dharma but is not focused exclusively on the teaching and practice of the Primal Vow, this can influence his students and lead them astray. A teacher, but also any follower, must be an example of exclusive reliance on Amida Buddha and the true teaching about Him. What is in one's heart and mind can influence one's fellow practitioners for better or for worse.

Honen said:

"Abandoning the miscellaneous practices and performing the exclusive practice of the recitation of Nembutsu are in accordance with the heart of Amida Buddha."[128]

Miscellaneous practices are any Buddhist practice except the Nembutsu of faith. These other practices were not mentioned in the Primal Vow, so they are called like this.

He also said:

"Sentient beings in this defiled world who aspire for birth in the Pure Land during the period of the decline of the Dharma (Dharma ending age) should have no other

---

[128] Honen Shonin, An Outline of the Doctrine for Birth in the Pure Land.*The Promise of Amida Buddha - Honen's Path to Bliss*; English translation of the Genko edition of the works of Honen Shonin - *Collected Teachings of Kurodani Shonin: The Japanese Anthology (Wago Toroku)*, translated by Joji Atone and Yoko Hayashi, Wisdom Publications, Boston, 2011, p.113

practice but the practice of reciting Nembutsu. They should, in compliance with the guidance of Master Shan-tao, enter the gate of the single-hearted and exclusive practice of Nembutsu.
However, I regret to say that there are very few who enter that gate with earnest hearts focused solely on Nembutsu. This is because some are attracted to other Buddhist practices, and others do not take the merits of Nembutsu seriously enough. I suppose that this must be the reason for the small number of people who profoundly believe in birth in the Pure Land, who realize this profound aspiration."[129]

"*The genuine heart refers to worshiping only Amida Buddha and to reciting His name wholeheartedly and exclusively without worshiping other Buddhas and observing other practices."*[130]

All Buddhas are worthy of worship but if we want to reach the specific Pure Land of Sukhavati we must be focused on the Master of that land. If we want to go from

---

[129] Honen Shonin, An Outline of Nembutsu. *The Promise of Amida Buddha - Honen's Path to Bliss*; English translation of the Genko edition of the works of Honen Shonin - *Collected Teachings of Kurodani Shonin: The Japanese Anthology (Wago Toroku)*, translated by Joji Atone and Yoko Hayashi, Wisdom Publications, Boston, 2011, p.142

[130] Honen Shonin, An Outline of Nembutsu. *The Promise of Amida Buddha - Honen's Path to Bliss*; English translation of the Genko edition of the works of Honen Shonin - *Collected Teachings of Kurodani Shonin: The Japanese Anthology (Wago Toroku)*, translated by Joji Atone and Yoko Hayashi, Wisdom Publications, Boston, 2011, p.146

point A to point B, we follow the direct course between these two, not the direction to point C. If we desire birth in the Pure Land, we follow the instructions of Amida: entrust only to Him and say only His Name. We should accept that Amida knows better than us the road to His own Pure Land, so we must stick with the instructions of His Primal Vow. Unfortunately, those who feel the need to do something else beside the Nembutsu are actually doubting the efficacy of the Name of Amida Buddha in bringing their birth in the Pure Land:

"Although it would seem not to be a hindrance for birth in the Pure Land to perform practices in addition to Nembutsu, on closer scrutiny, one can see that to do so belies a lingering doubt about the certain attainment of birth in the Pure Land through Nembutsu."[131]

The sure sign of faith (shinjin) is to be completely satisfied with the Nembutsu. Unlike followers of miscellaneous practices, Jodo Shinshu followers are madly in love with Amida and have only His Name on their lips.
Namo Amida Bu

---

[131] Honen Shonin, An Outline of Nembutsu. *The Promise of Amida Buddha - Honen's Path to Bliss*; English translation of the Genko edition of the works of Honen Shonin - *Collected Teachings of Kurodani Shonin: The Japanese Anthology (Wago Toroku)*, translated by Joji Atone and Yoko Hayashi, Wisdom Publications, Boston, 2011, p.147

Just say the Nembutsu without adding anything to it

"Once a devotee from the Chinzei district came up to Kyoto to visit Honen at his cottage.
Before meeting him, he asked one of Honen's disciples if it was a good thing to meditate upon the Buddha's signs of eminence while one is repeating the Nembutsu. The reply was that it was an excellent thing to do.

Honen who was sitting in the adjoining room before the Buddha's image, overheard the conversation. He opened the sliding door and remarked, 'I don't think so. It is as Zendo (Master Shan-tao) says, 'If a single one of the sentient beings in the ten quarters of the world should fail to be born into the Pure Land through calling of my Name at least ten times, then I refuse for myself the perfect Enlightenment of Buddhahood. Now the fact is that He did become a Buddha and now exists as one. So, from this we are perfectly sure that His Great Primal Vow was not in vain. If therefore any sentient being now does call upon His Name, he shall certainly attain Ojo (birth in the Pure Land). No matter how much we may meditate upon the Buddha, we cannot do it in the perfect way as Shakyamuni explained it (in the Contemplation Sutra). So, the only thing for us to do is to put our trust deeply in the Primal Vow itself, and call upon the sacred Name with our lips. This is the one and only way to practice religion.[132]*'"*[133]

---

[132] Words in brackets are my own.

[133] Honen the Buddhist Saint - His Life and Teachings, volume III, compiled by imperial order, translation by Rev Ryugaku Ishizuka

Commentary:
We should always come back to the Primal Vow whenever we have a question. So, where in the Primal Vow did Amida mention that we should say His Name while meditating upon His signs of eminence? Nowhere! The inquiry in the above passage was made on the basis of the thirteen contemplations in the *Contemplation Sutra* which is a provisional teaching for those who still cling to their self-power. However, it has absolutely no connection with the Nembutsu of the Primal Vow or the Nembutsu of Amida centered Power. In His Primal Vow, Amida asked us to entrust to Him and say His Name *"perhaps even ten times"* which means that our relaxed saying of Nembutsu (without being obsessed with numbers) should be an expression of faith in His Power. It is a simple saying of the Name without adding anything to it. The Primal Vow mentions a simple saying of the Name in faith because Amida wanted this to be the easiest Path among all Dharma methods. As long as He didn't consider adding anything else except the saying of His Name in faith and the wish to be born in His Pure Land, why do we think we are smarter than Him by adding something else? Certainly, the Primal Vow does not need any improvement.

More than this, Amida linked this Path of birth in the Pure Land with His own attainment of perfect Enlightenment:

---

and Rev Harper Havelock Coates, The Society for the Publication of Sacred Books of the World, Kyoto, 1949, p. 442-443

"If, when I attain Buddhahood, sentient beings of the ten quarters who sincerely entrust themselves to me, desire to be born in my land, and say my Name perhaps even ten times, should not be born there, may I not attain the supreme Enlightenment." (The Primal Vow)

As Amida actually attained Enlightenment, we should have no doubt that to say His Name in faith leads to birth there. A Buddha never breaks His promise and He is the only one to know the karmic causes for birth in His own Pure Land, so have trust in Amida and do exclusively what He told you to do. Those who think that the requirements of Amida in His Primal Vow are not enough to cause birth in His Pure Land, actually doubt His wisdom and do not have genuine faith.

The thirteen contemplations are provisional practices while the Nembutsu of faith is the main Gate to the Pure Land

*"Jogan Shonin (1168-1251) thus stated: 'Someone said to Honen Shonin, 'The perception of the physical features of Amida Buddha is taught in the Contemplation Sutra. Should even Nembutsu practitioners observe this meditative practice?' Honen Shonin replied: 'I, Genku, also observed **such a futile practice** at the beginning, but I do not practice it now. I recite the Nembutsu with implicit belief in attaining birth in the Pure Land.'"*[134]

Commentary:
Why did Honen Shonin regard the thirteen contemplations in the above-mentioned sutra to be a futile practice? And if he regarded them so, why were they mentioned there?

The answer to the first question is that the thirteen contemplations and the perception of the physical features of Amida Buddha are NOT found in His Primal Vow where only faith, Nembutsu of faith and wish to be born in the Pure Land are mentioned. Because they are not part of the Primal Vow, it means they do not constitute the main intention of Amida and are not the

---

[134] *The Promise of Amida Buddha - Honen's Path to Bliss*; English translation of the Genko edition of the works of Honen Shonin - *Collected Teachings of Kurodani Shonin: The Japanese Anthology (Wago Toroku)*, translated by Joji Atone and Yoko Hayashi, Wisdom Publications, Boston, 2011, p.304-305

cause of birth in the fulfilled land (center) of the Pure Land where we immediately become Buddhas.

As to why they were mentioned by Shakyamuni in the *Contemplation Sutra*, the answer is that those thirteen contemplations are related to the 19th Vow which represents the Path Amida designed for those still not ready to fully entrust themselves to His Power but still think there is something they need to do by themselves in order to obtain birth there. Please refer to my detailed explanations of *The Path of the 19th Vow and the explicit and implicit (hidden) meaning of the Contemplation Sutra* as well as the chapter dedicated to the 19th Vow from my *Commentary on the Sutra on the Buddha of Infinite Life*.
Thus, the thirteen contemplations and the *Contemplation Sutra* itself are provisional teachings, while the *Larger Sutra* where the Primal Vow is mentioned, is the true intention of Amida and Shakyamuni.

Those who seriously follow such practices as the thirteen contemplations will be born in the Border land of the Pure Land where due to their lack of complete trust in Amida's Power will stay for some time until the sin of doubt is expiated, while those who enter the Pure Land through the Gate of the Primal Vow by saying the Nembutsu of faith *("Nembutsu with implicit faith")* will instantly attain Buddhahood upon birth in the center of the Pure Land, thus being able at once to benefit all sentient beings.

Also, due to the difficulty of the practice of the thirteen contemplations very few can actually do them correctly, so why bother ourselves with them when we have the Name of Amida which can be said by anybody and which does not even depend on us to be effective! When we are born in the Pure Land, we'll be able to clearly see all its splendors, including the glorious features of Amida, so there is no need to bother with that now when His main instruction is to simply say the Nembutsu of faith.

The need for oral instructions by a true teacher

Honen Shonin said:

"A man who reads about the doctrines of the Jodo (Pure Land) without receiving oral instruction will miss the thing really necessary to the attainment of Ojo (birth in the Pure Land). Men of high station such as Nagarjuna and Vasubandhu, and on the other hand, men of the lowest rank of common latter-day sinners guilty of the ten evil deeds and the five deadly sins, used to be the object of Shakyamuni Buddha's exhortations to enter the Land of Perfect Bliss. Now we, common men of the lowest class, when we hear the Buddha exhorting good men at once begin to depreciate ourselves and to think that we cannot be born into the Pure Land, and so we actually by our doubts prevent ourselves from reaching that birth after death. The main thing, then, is that we clearly distinguish between the teaching intended for the good, and that applicable to the evil like ourselves. If we are so minded, our faith in the certainty of our own Birth will become assured, and through the power of the Buddha's Primal Vow we shall accomplish our birth into that land at death."[135]

---

[135] Honen the Buddhist Saint - His Life and Teachings, volume III, compiled by imperial order, translation by Rev Ryugaku Ishizuka and Rev Harper Havelock Coates, The Society for the Publication of Sacred Books of the World, Kyoto, 1949, p. 394

Commentary:
I often meet with people who, after hearing about the Pure Land teaching, they go directly to the sutras or to difficult texts like *Kyogyoshinsho* and get stuck in various phrases that seem to contradict each other. It is said that one should not give swords to youngsters because they can easily hurt themselves with them. In the same way, beginners not yet settled in faith and with a chaotic mind should not study the sutras and other sacred texts without proper guidance by a true teacher. I don't deny that some might have the good karma of quickly understanding the essentials of our tradition by themselves, but those are very few when compared with the majority who need help to clear their doubts and misunderstandings.

Our Path is easy, but the obstacles people often have when getting in touch with it come from their own minds that are used to a totally different paradigm than that of the Pure Land teaching. It is hard to get over the mental habit of thinking that you have to do something to be worthy of a certain goal. This can be useful in worldly life but is totally useless on the Nembutsu Path where we "let go and let Amida". Due to our habitual tendency to not forgive those who wronged us and not being able to forgive ourselves too, we tend to think that it is not right for evil people like ourselves and others to be saved so easily by Amida. However, Infinite Compassion has nothing to do with our limited conception of good and evil, and Amida Buddha is not a judge but a loving Parent and Savior.

What mother would refuse to save her child from drowning because he is evil? For our unenlightened eyes people are just good and evil, worthy or not worthy of salvation, but for Amida Buddha we are all suffering children wandering in samsara. Where we see good and evil, He sees suffering beings that must be saved. Many of us *"discuss only good and evil, leaving Amida's benevolence out of consideration"*[136], as it is said in Tannisho, forgetting that *"the Primal Vow of Amida makes no distinction between people young and old, good and evil"* and that *"it is the Vow to save the person whose karmic evil is deep and grave and whose blind passions abound"*[137]. We forget that *"only shinjin (faith) is essential"*, but a true teacher will always remind this to us through his oral instructions and help us overcome our mental obstacles.

There is no need to compare ourselves with others and get depressed or discouraged because they are better than us. We should instead focus on our personal relation with Amida Buddha because His Primal Vow was made for each one of us in particular. This is the meaning of Shinran's words: *"when I deeply contemplate Amida's Compassionate Vow, I realize it was made only for me, Shinran."* Replace the word "Shinran", with your own name, and say, "when I deeply contemplate Amida's Compassionate Vow, I realize it was made only for me, John, Mary, Marc, etc." It is useless to worry or be

---

[136] *The Collected Works of Shinran*, Shin Buddhism Translation Series, Jodo Shinshu Hongwanji-ha, Kyoto, 1997, p.679
[137] *The Collected Works of Shinran*, Shin Buddhism Translation Series, Jodo Shinshu Hongwanji-ha, Kyoto, 1997, p.661

jealous that others are better than us when as long as one is not a Buddha yet, nobody can call oneself truly good.

Honen Shonin said:

"Do not be worrying as to whether your evil passions are strong or otherwise, or whether your sins are light or heavy. Only invoke Amida's Name with your lips, and let the conviction (shinjin/faith) accompany the sound of your voice, that you will of a certainty be born into the Pure Land."[138]

Shinran, his disciple, also said:

"As for me, I simply accept and entrust myself to what my revered teacher told me, 'Just say the Nembutsu and be saved by Amida'; nothing else is involved."[139]

Any true teacher will say the same and you need one to simplify your understanding and help you focus on Amida.

Namo Amida Bu

---

[138] Honen the Buddhist Saint - His Life and Teachings, volume III, compiled by imperial order, translation by Rev Ryugaku Ishizuka and Rev Harper Havelock Coates, The Society for the Publication of Sacred Books of the World, Kyoto, 1949, p. 395
[139] *The Collected Works of Shinran*, Shin Buddhism Translation Series, Jodo Shinshu Hongwanji-ha, Kyoto, 1997, p.662

Rev. Jōshō Adrian Cîrlea (Adrian Gheorghe Cîrlea) is the representative of Jodo Shinshu Buddhist Community from Romania and founder of Amidaji branch of Jodo Shinshu Buddhism (Amidaji International Temple).

Printed in Great Britain
by Amazon